It was a beautyfull foggy day...

Jaworzec
= Forest in the Fog

Landscape and Nature Photo Book

Series: In the Bieszczady Mountains

Photos by
Jacek Lidwin

Table of contents:

Text about Jaworzec 7

Beginning of photos 8

About author 49

Near Kalnica in the Bieszczady Mountains, in the valley through which the Wetlinka stream flows, there was a village inhabited by Boyko's. In 1947 they were forcibly displaced to the north and west of Poland. In 2012, the remains of the village were partially reconstructed and provided with information boards.

Currently there is a mountain shelter nearby. The surrounding mountains are covered with dense forest.

Photos were taken with a mobile phone in May 2017.

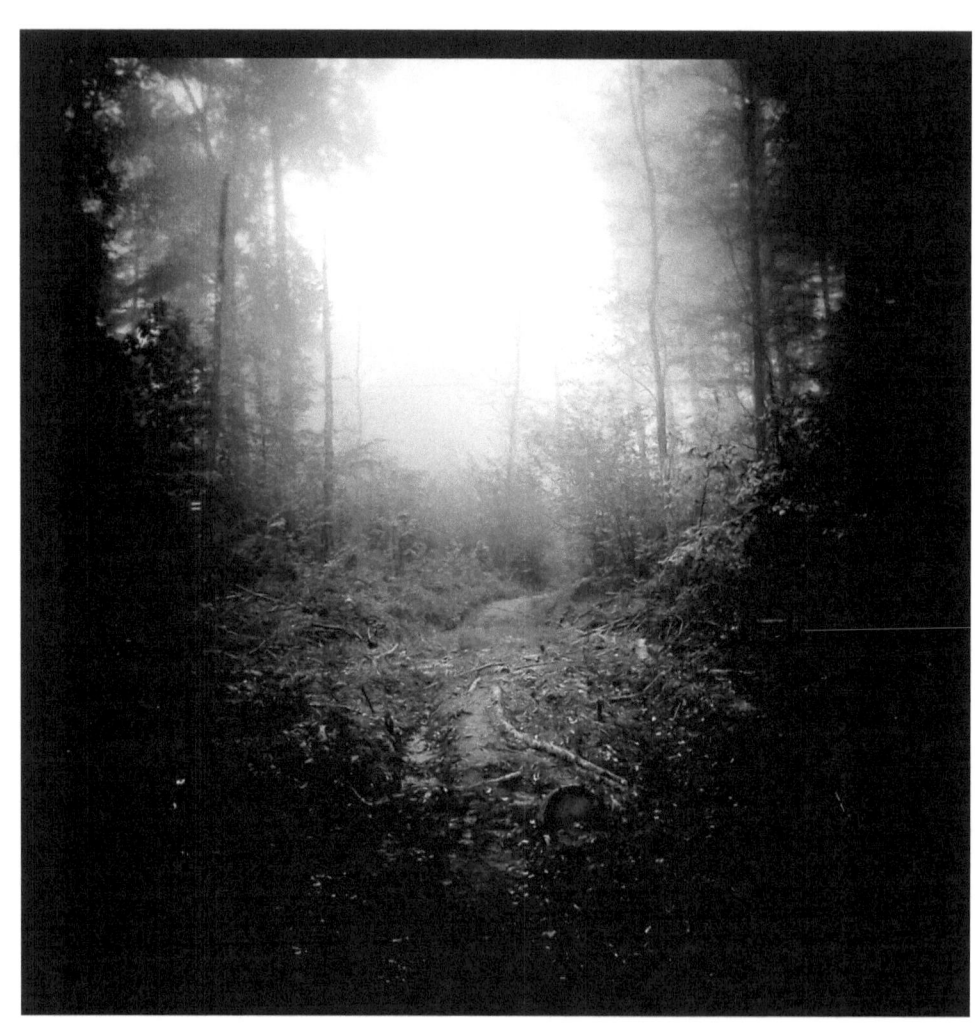

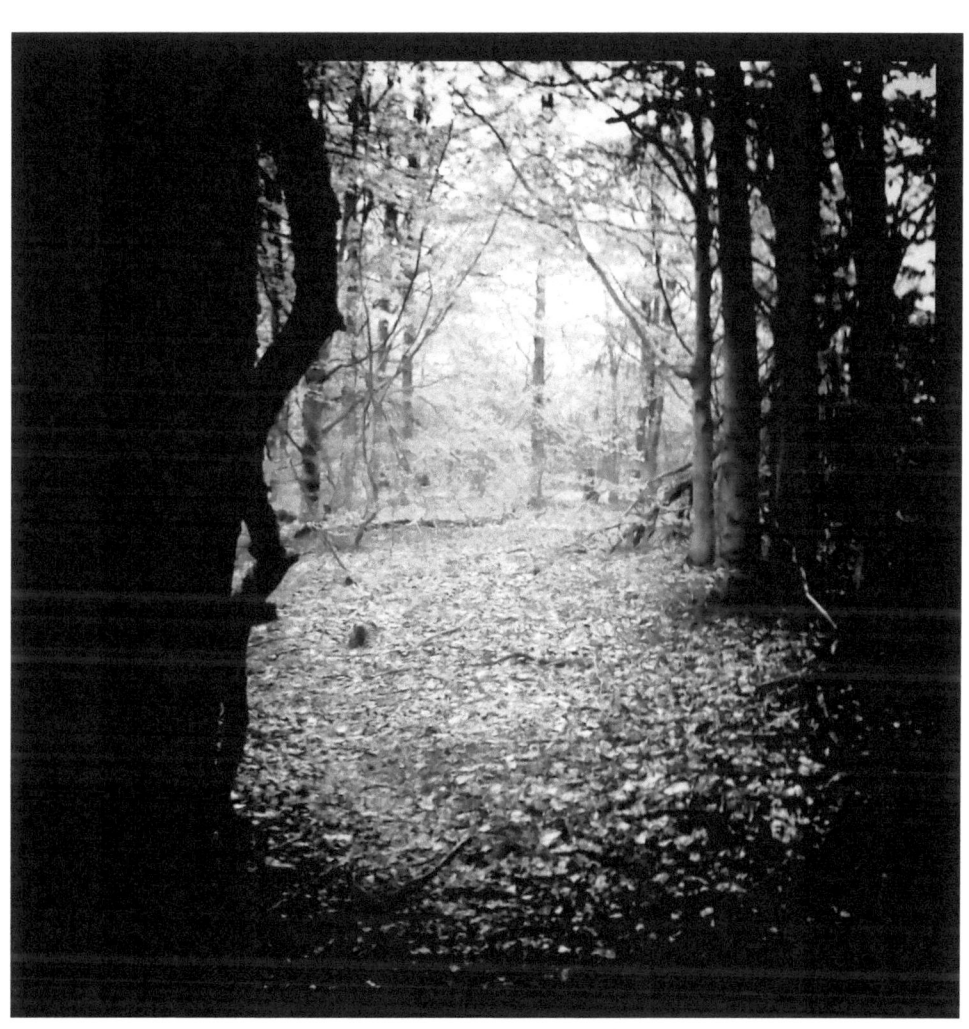

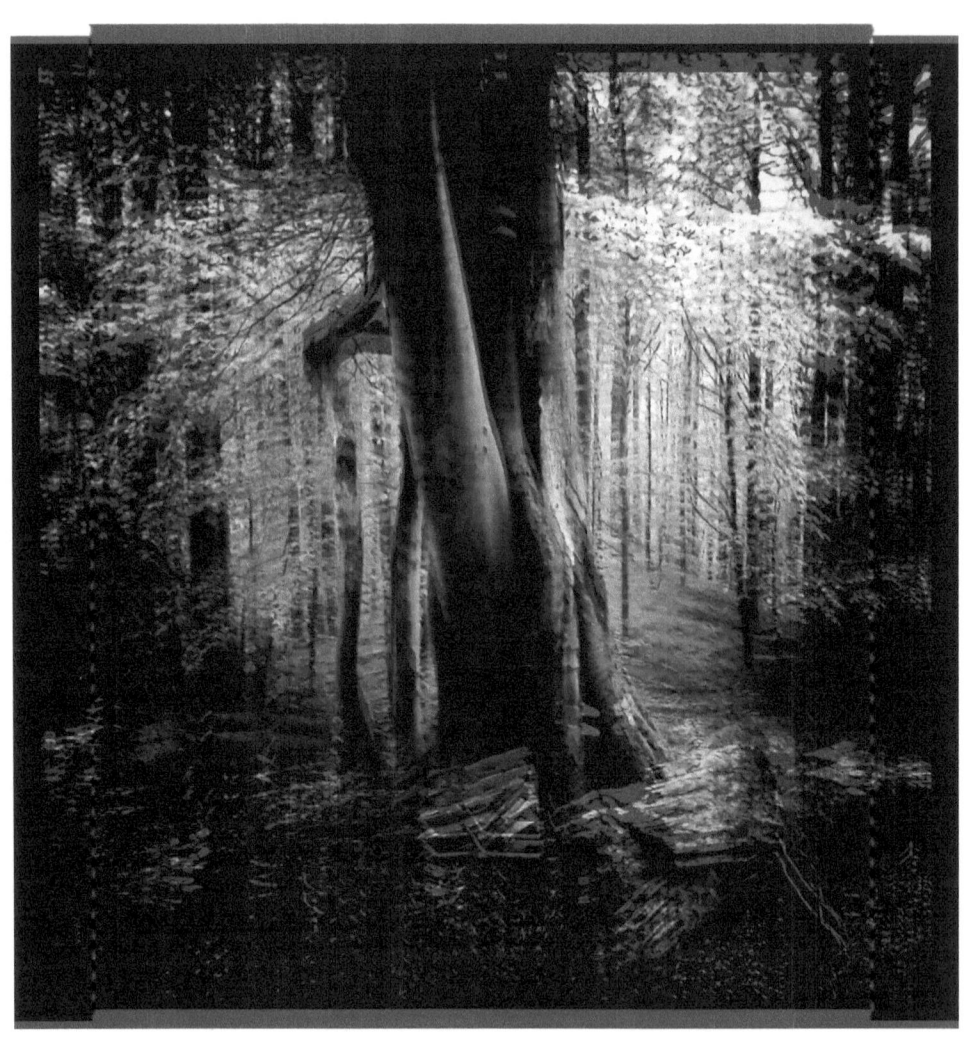

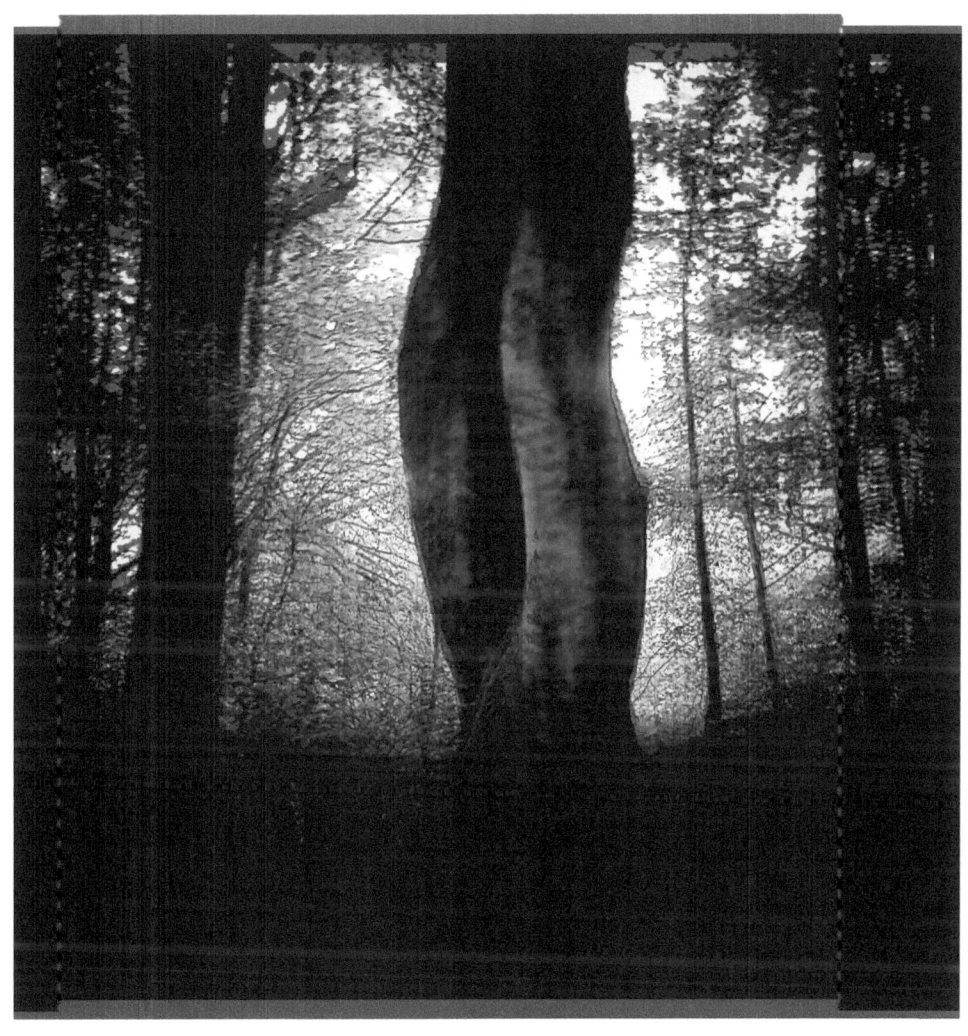

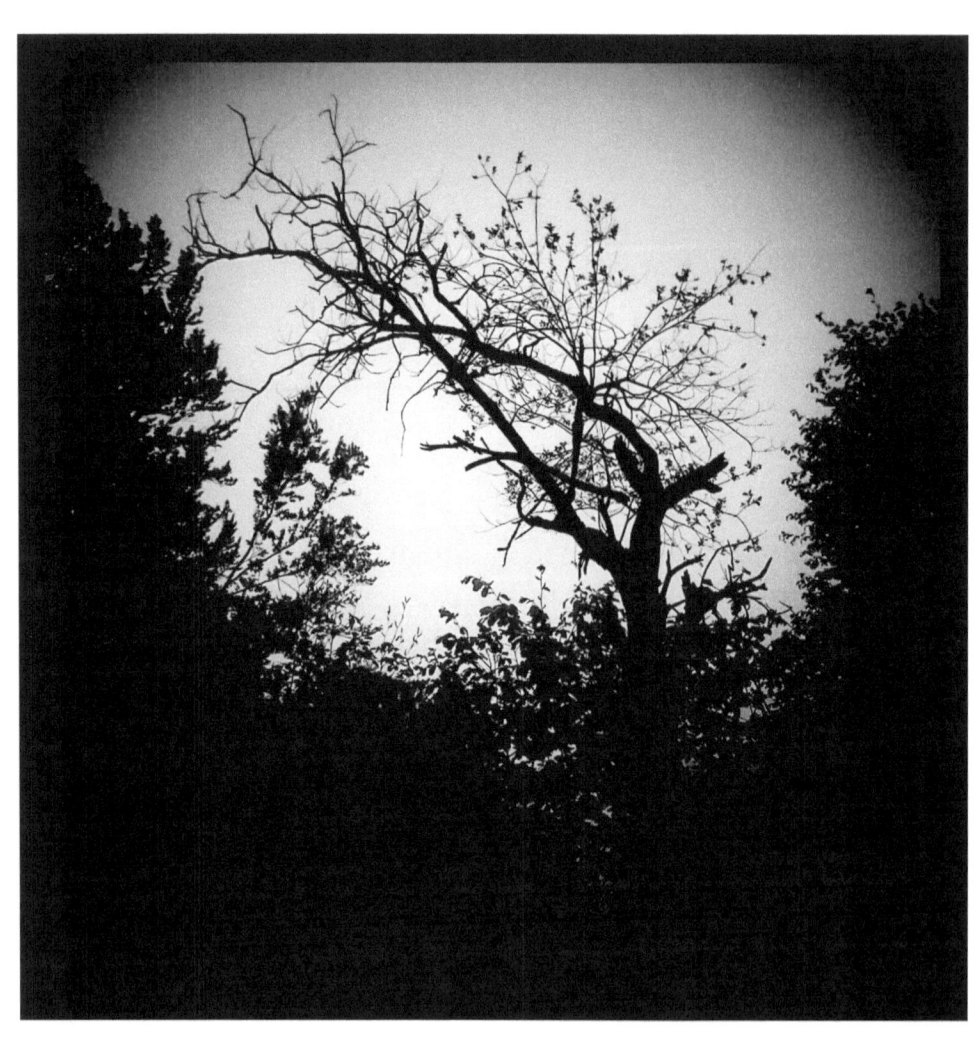

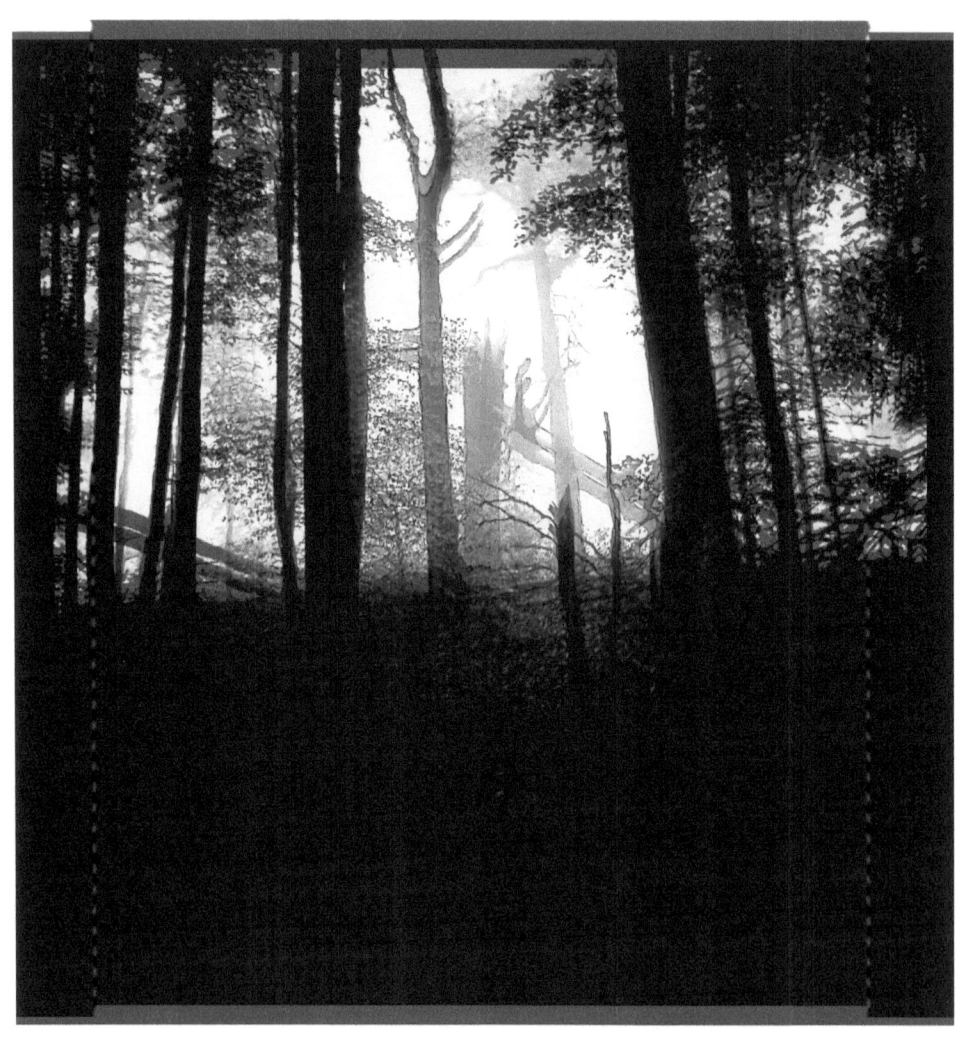

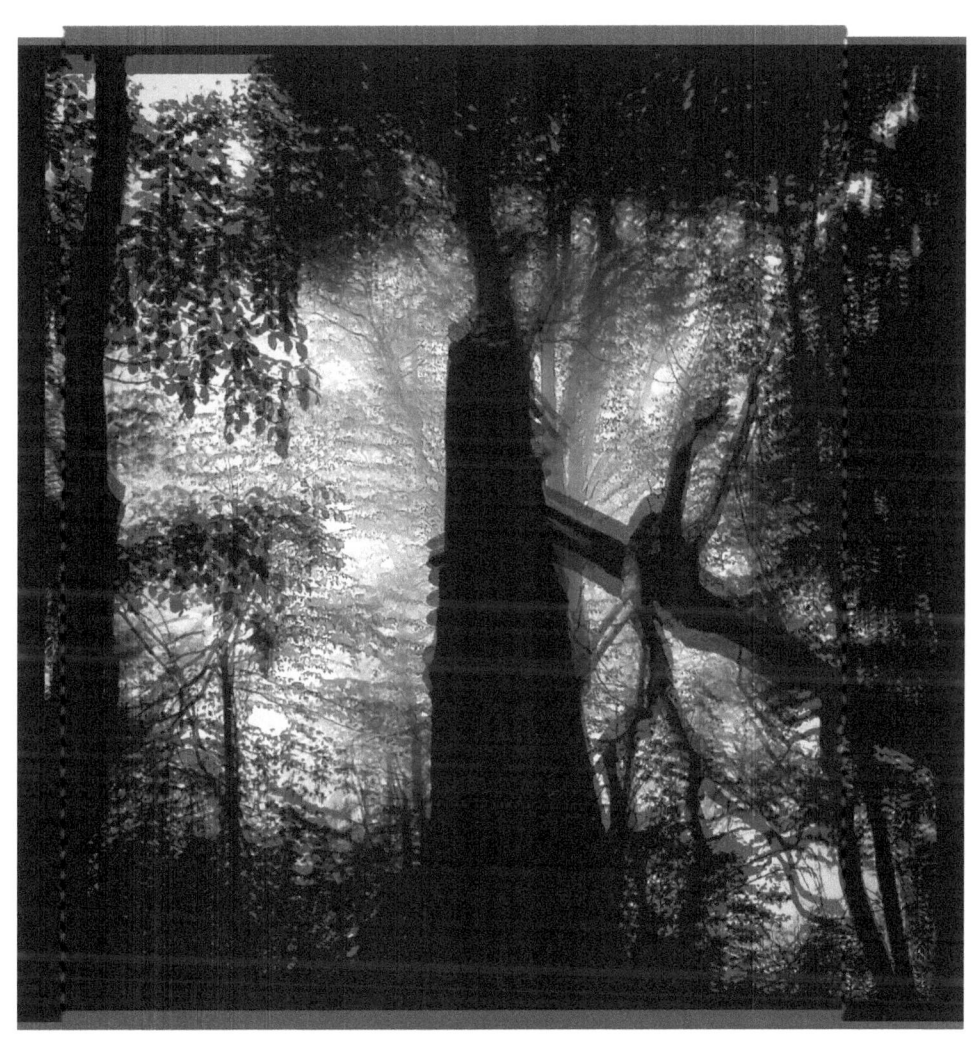

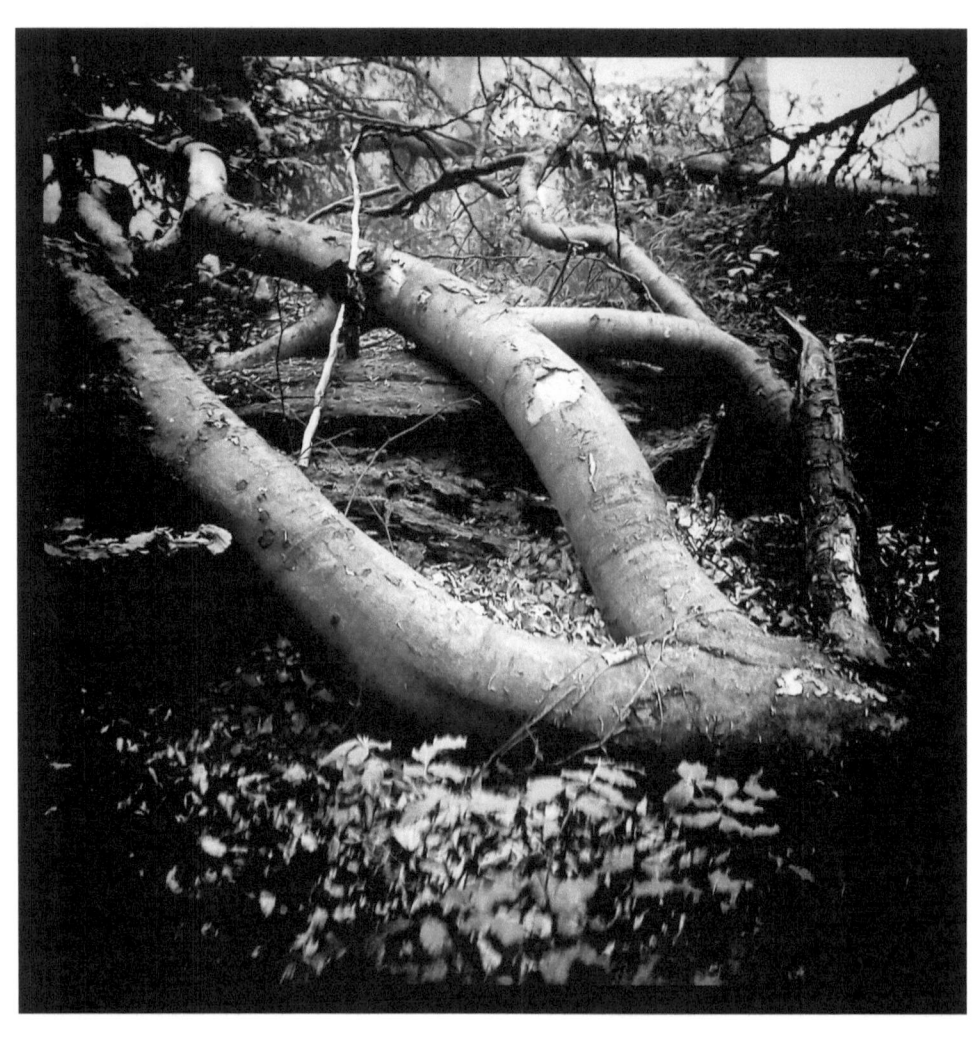

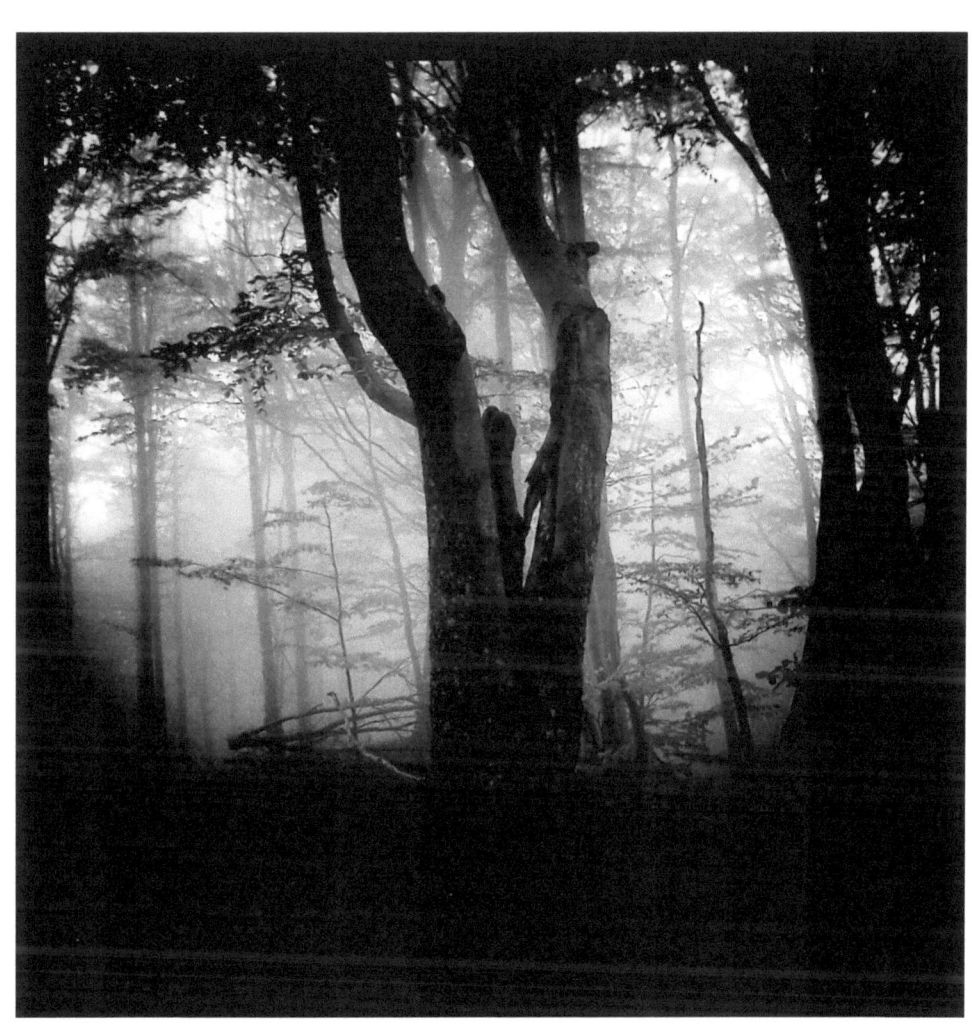

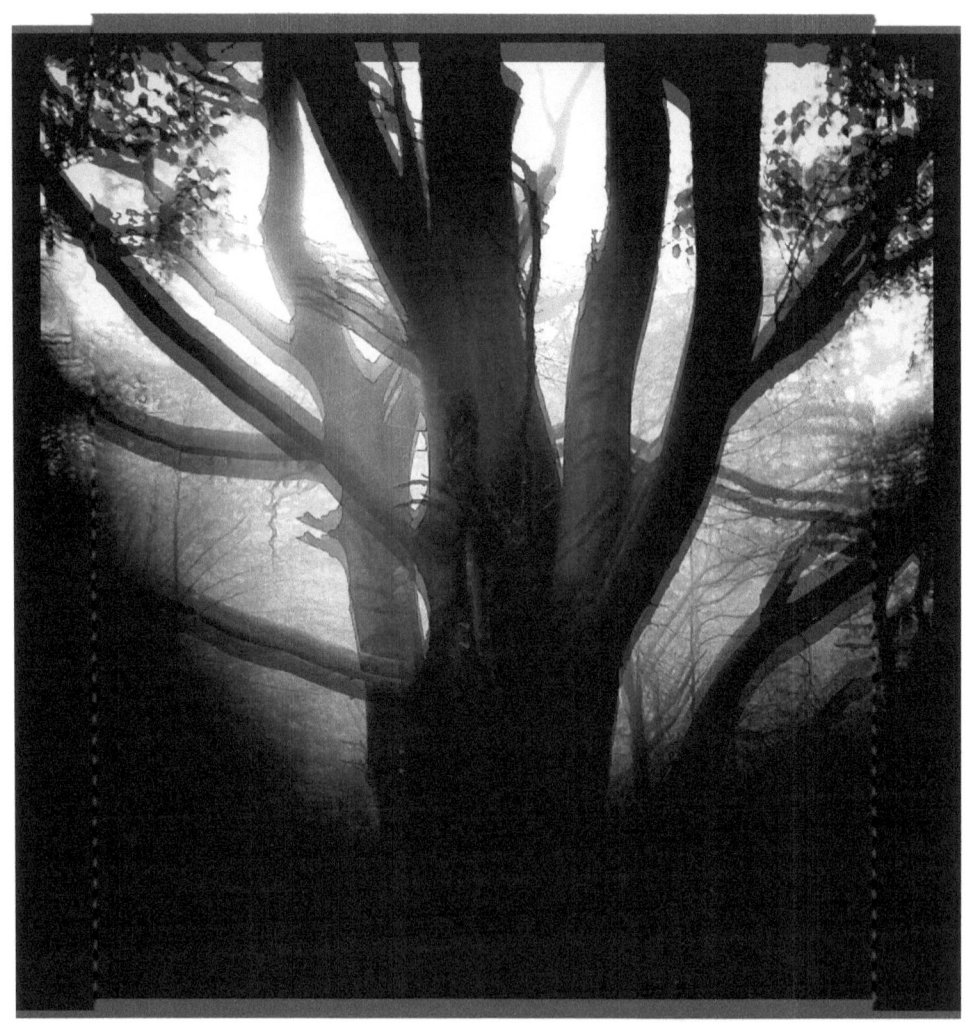

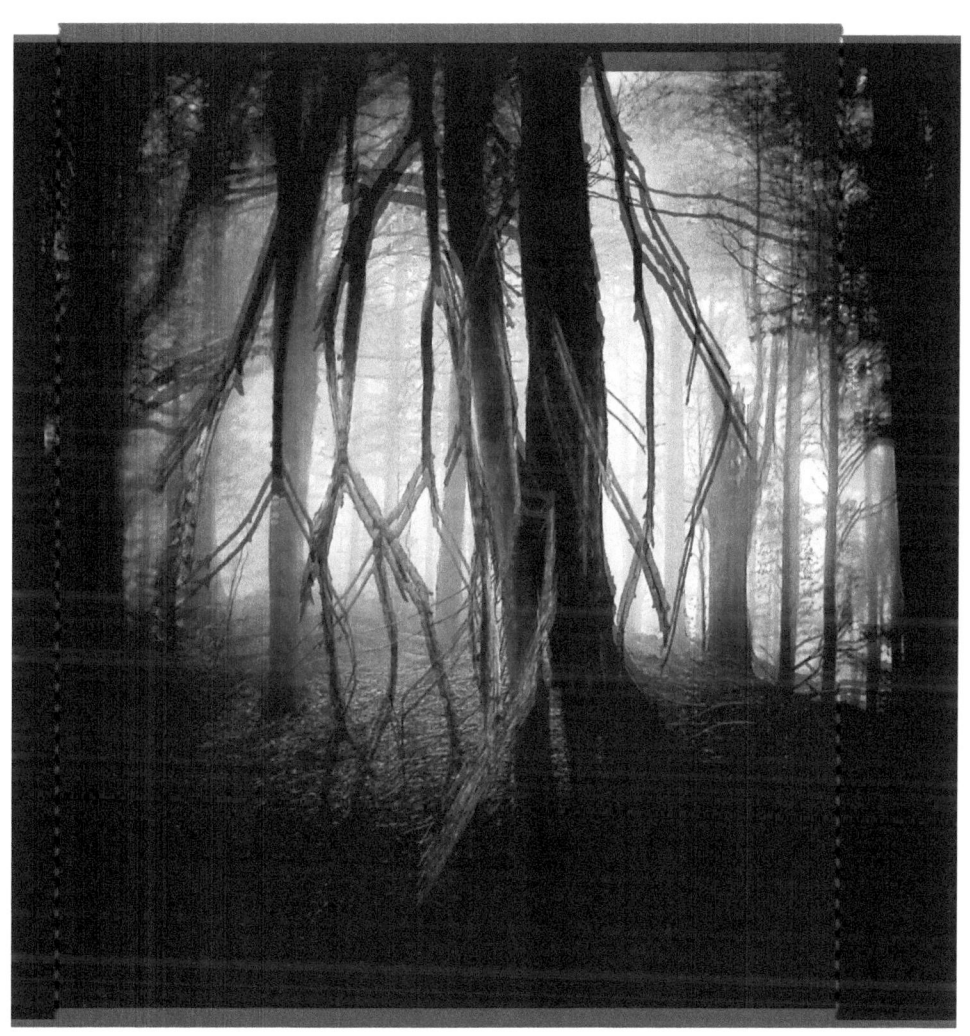

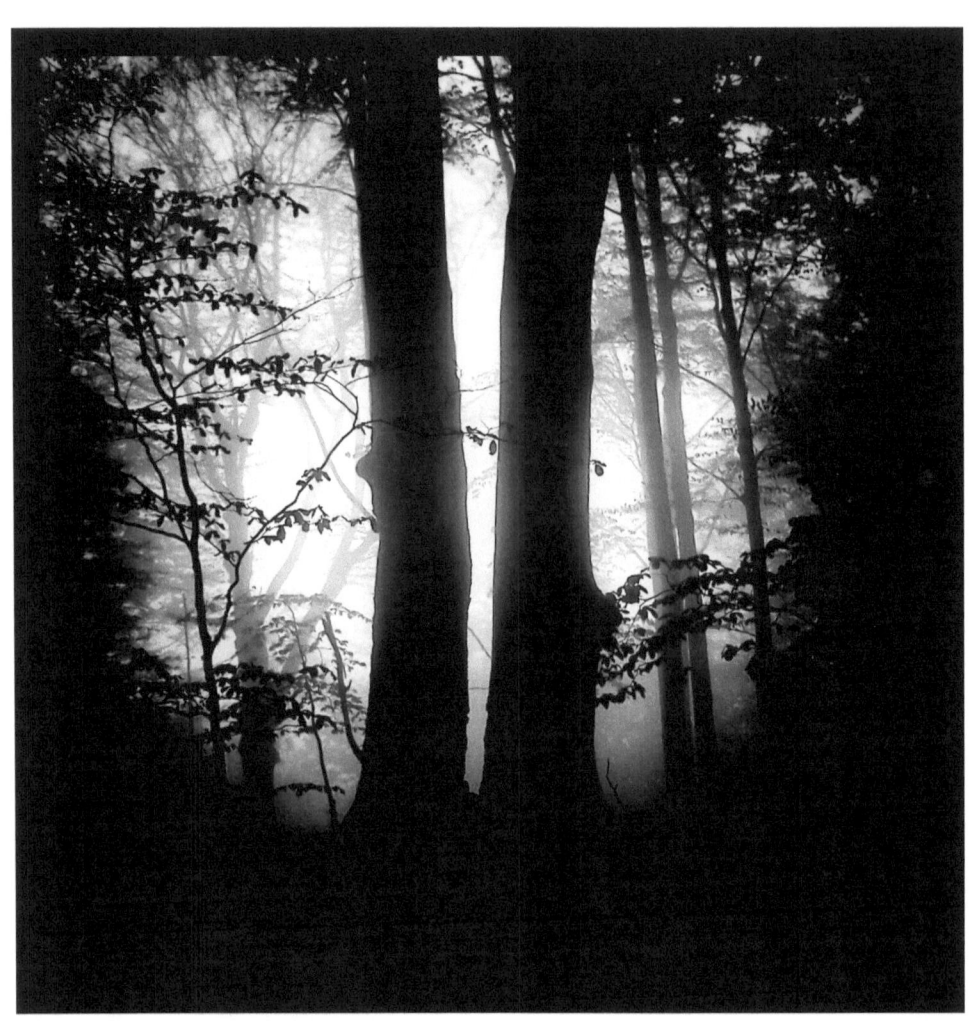

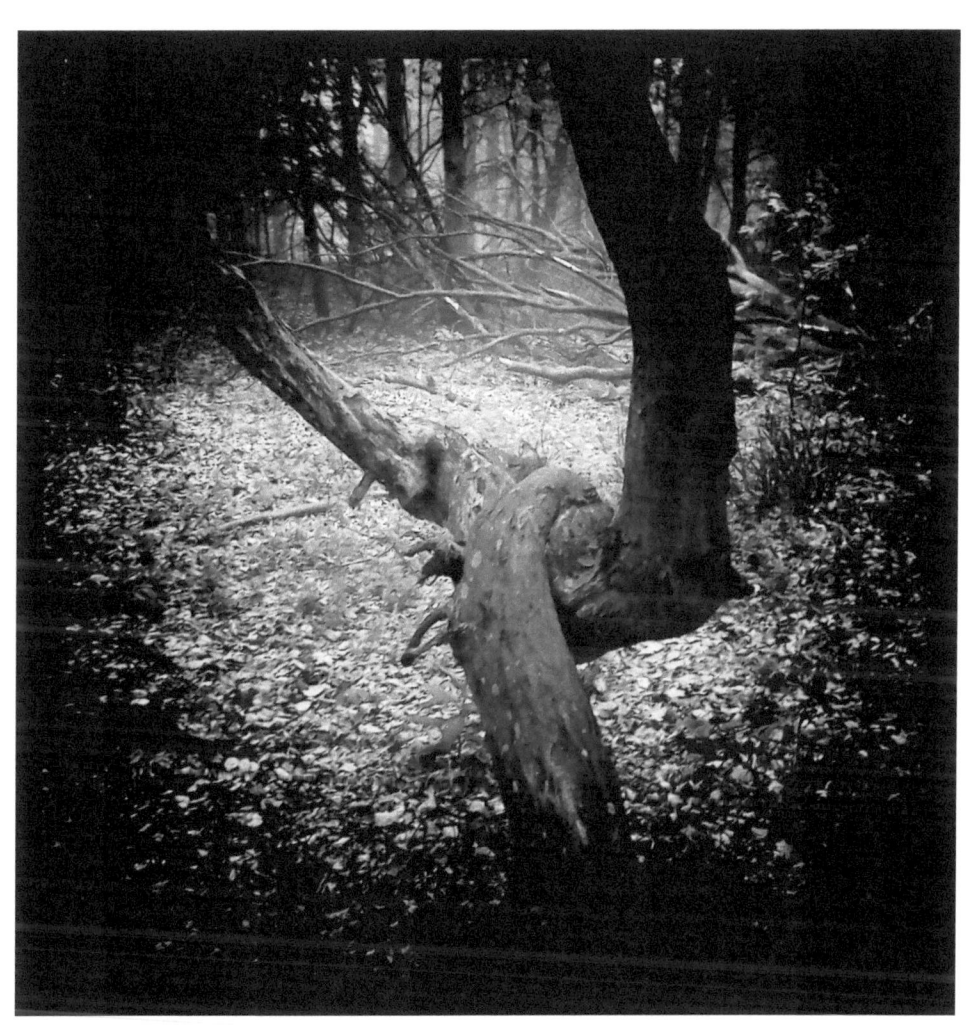

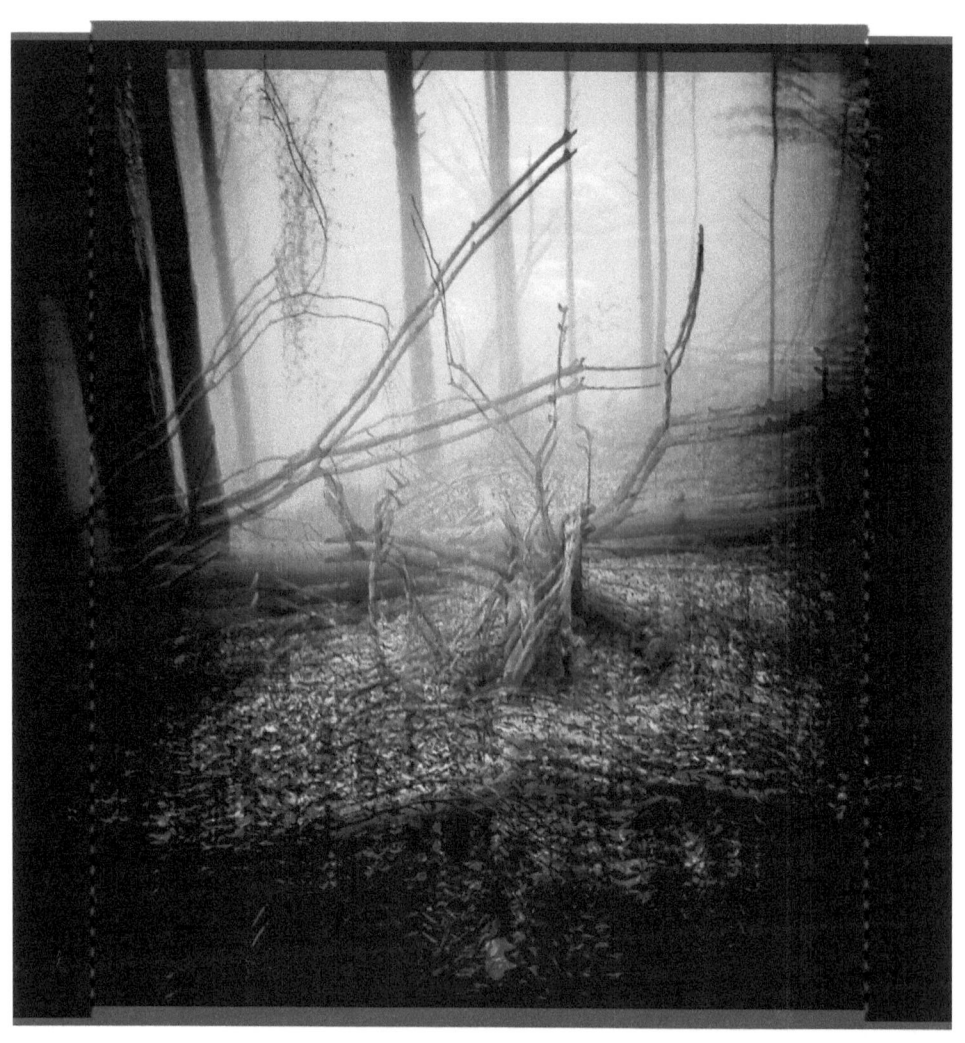

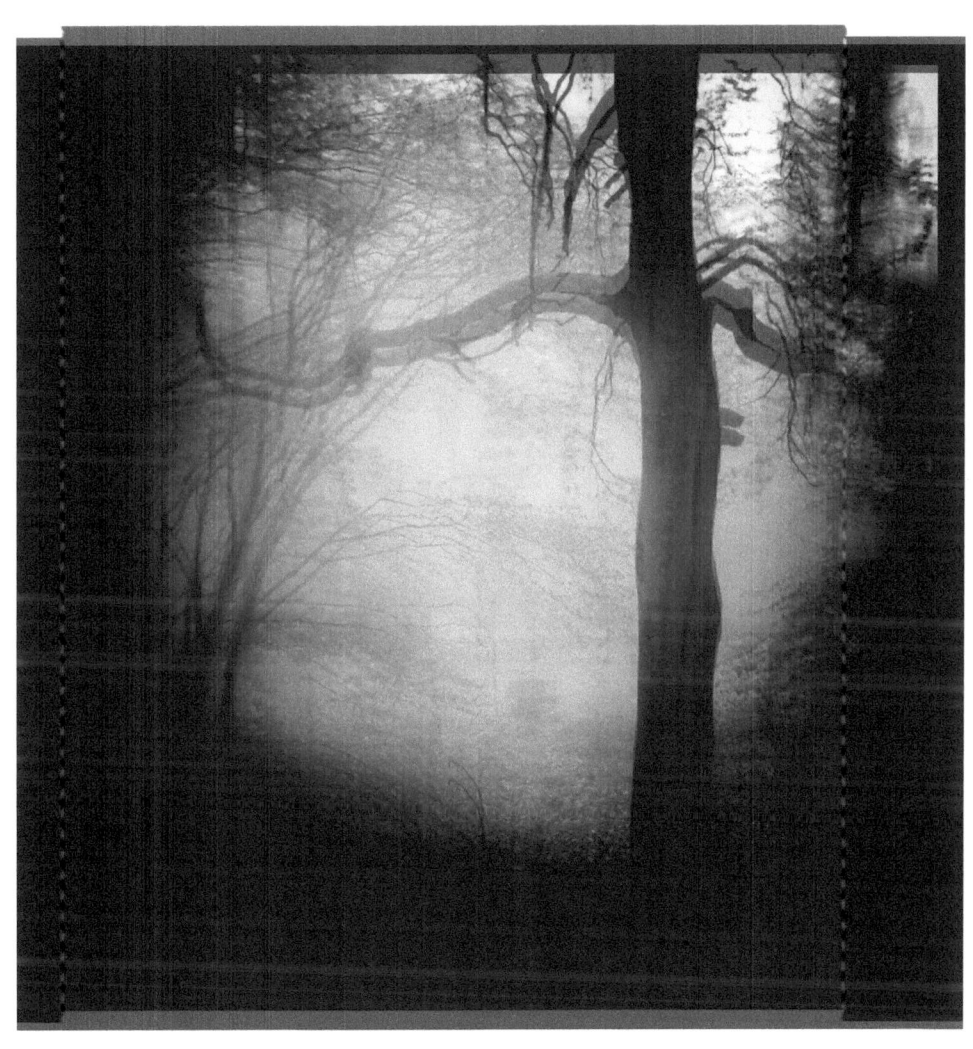

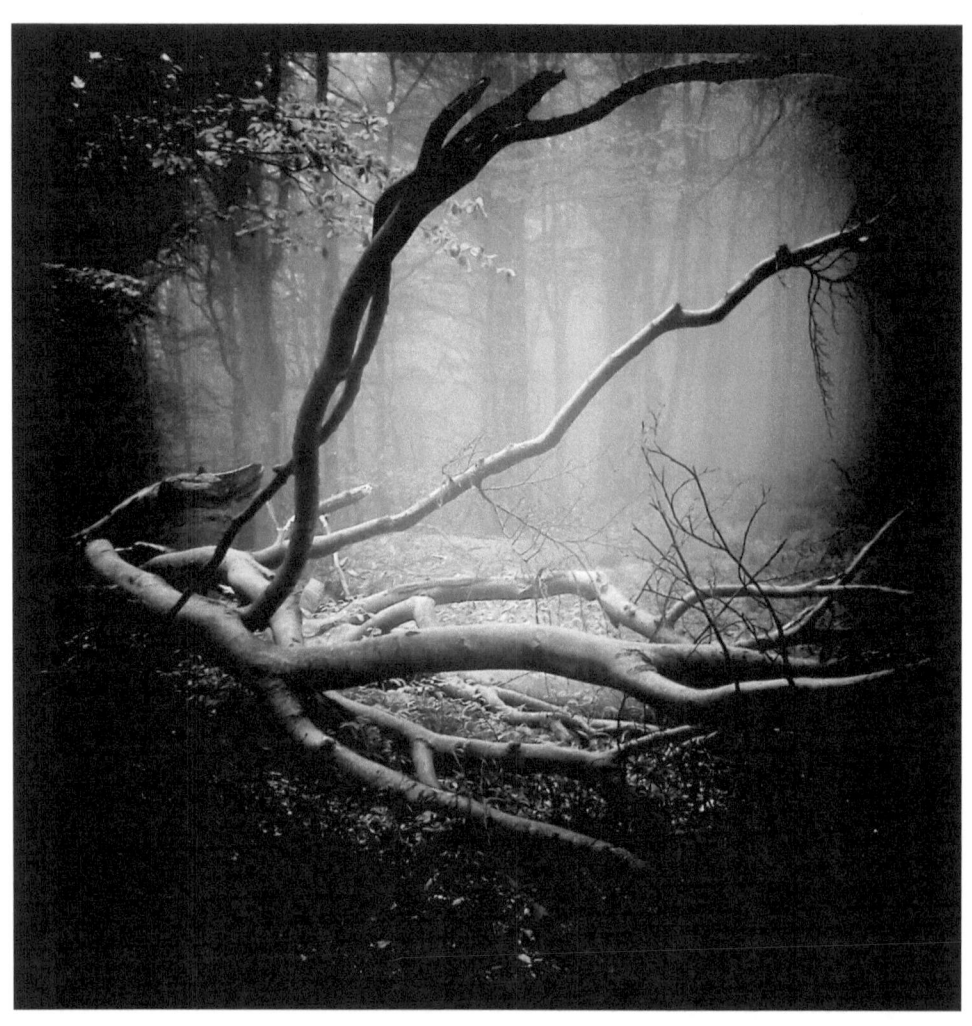

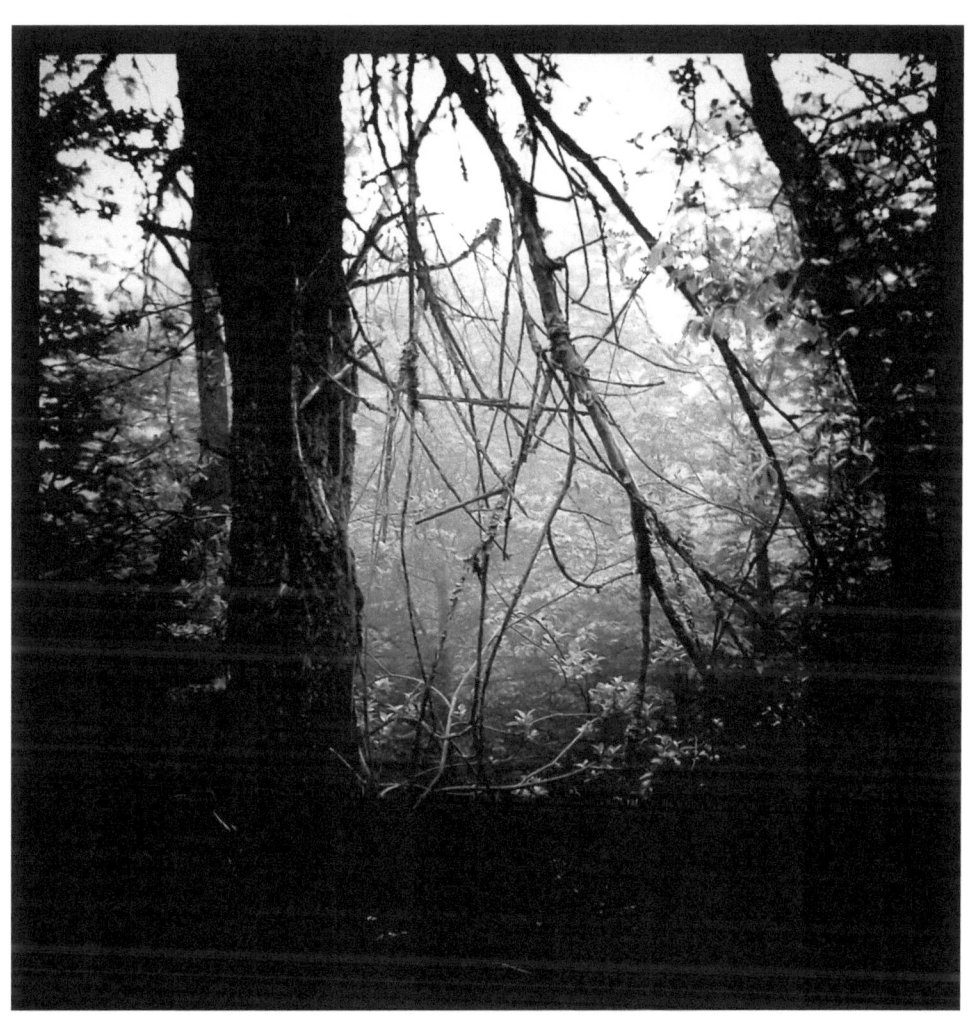

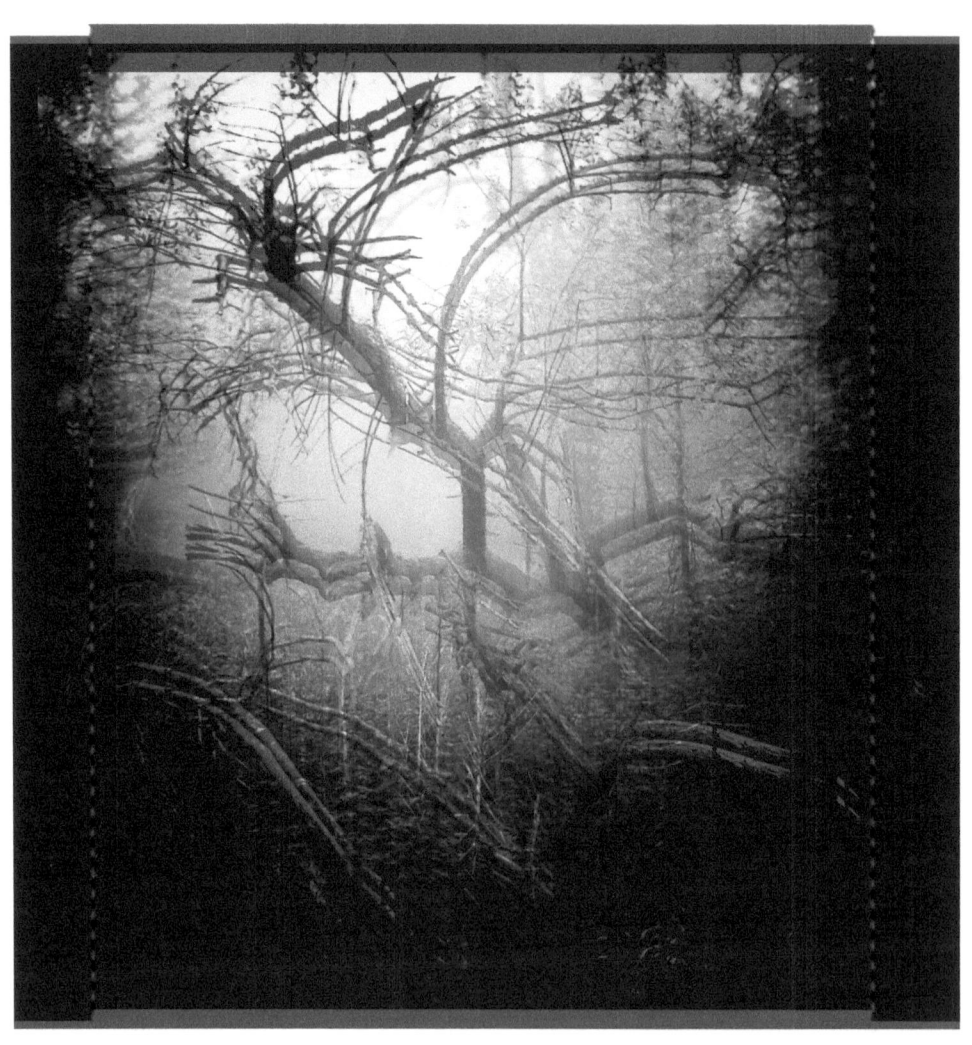

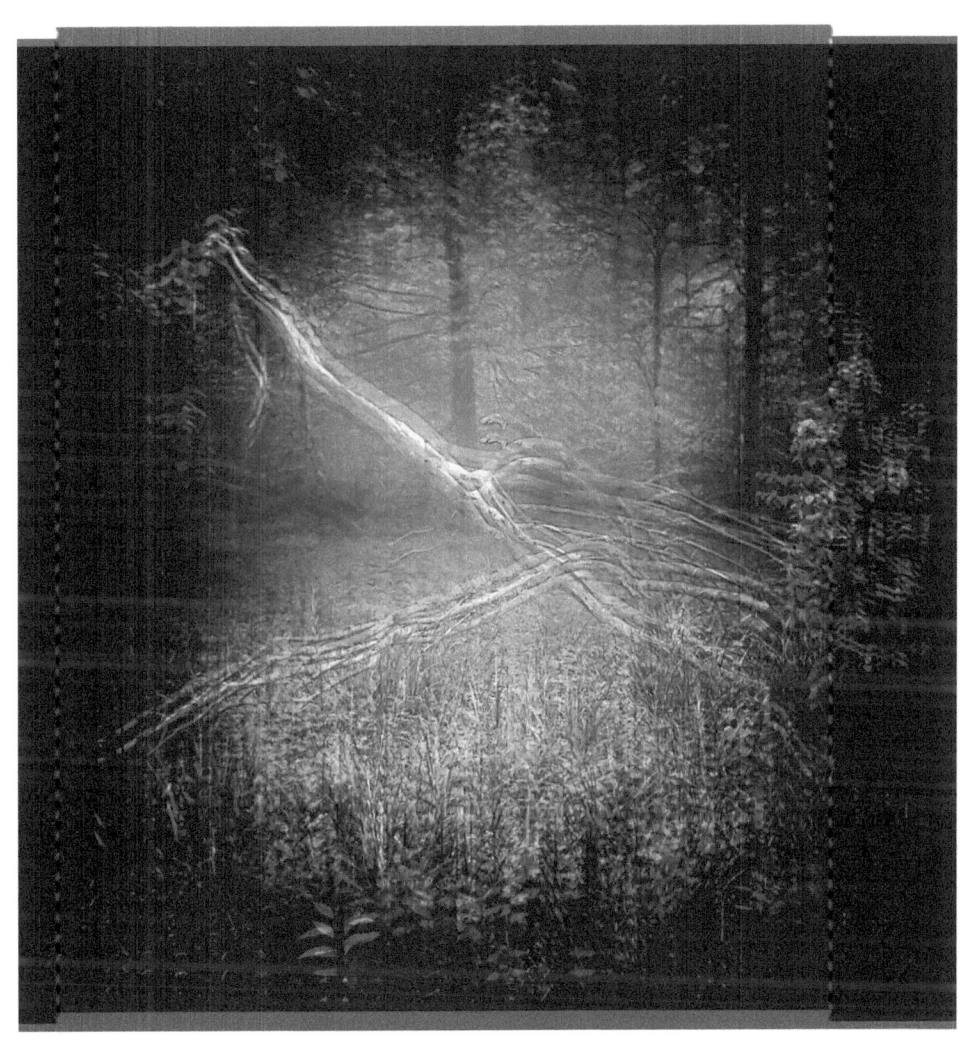

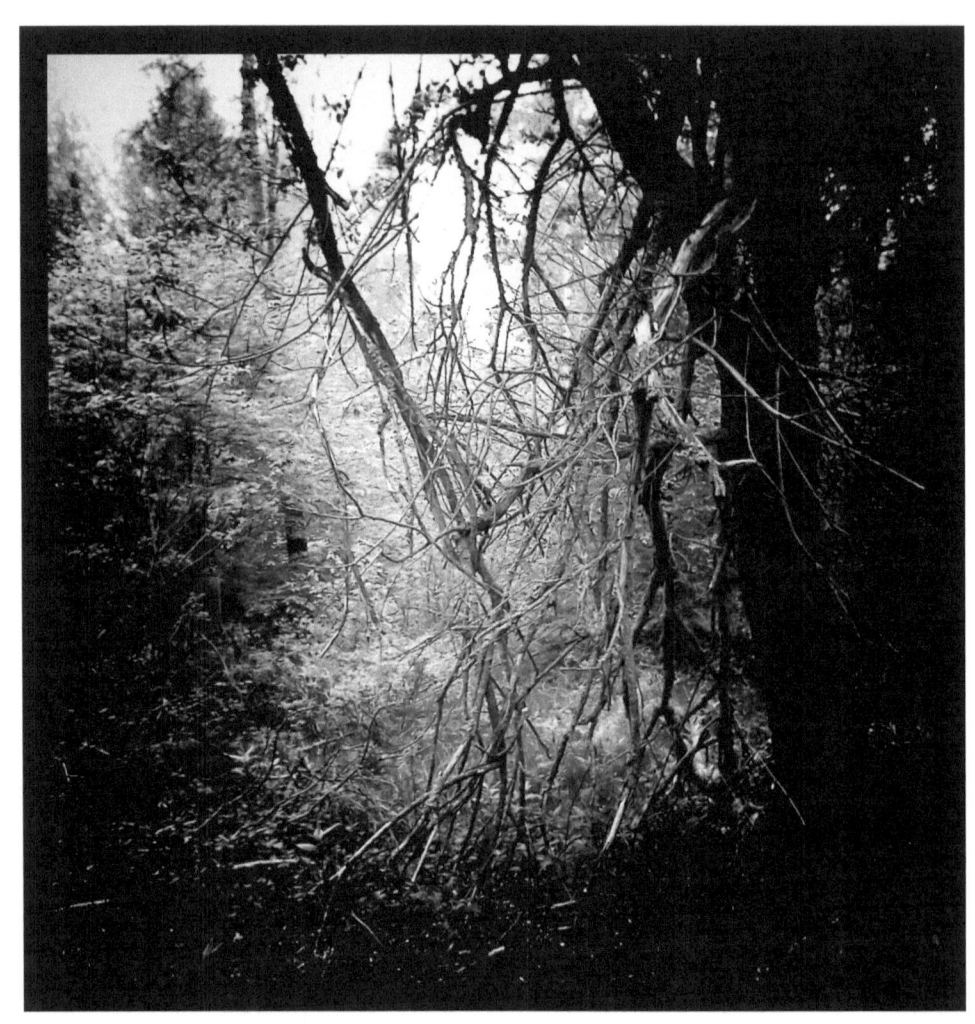

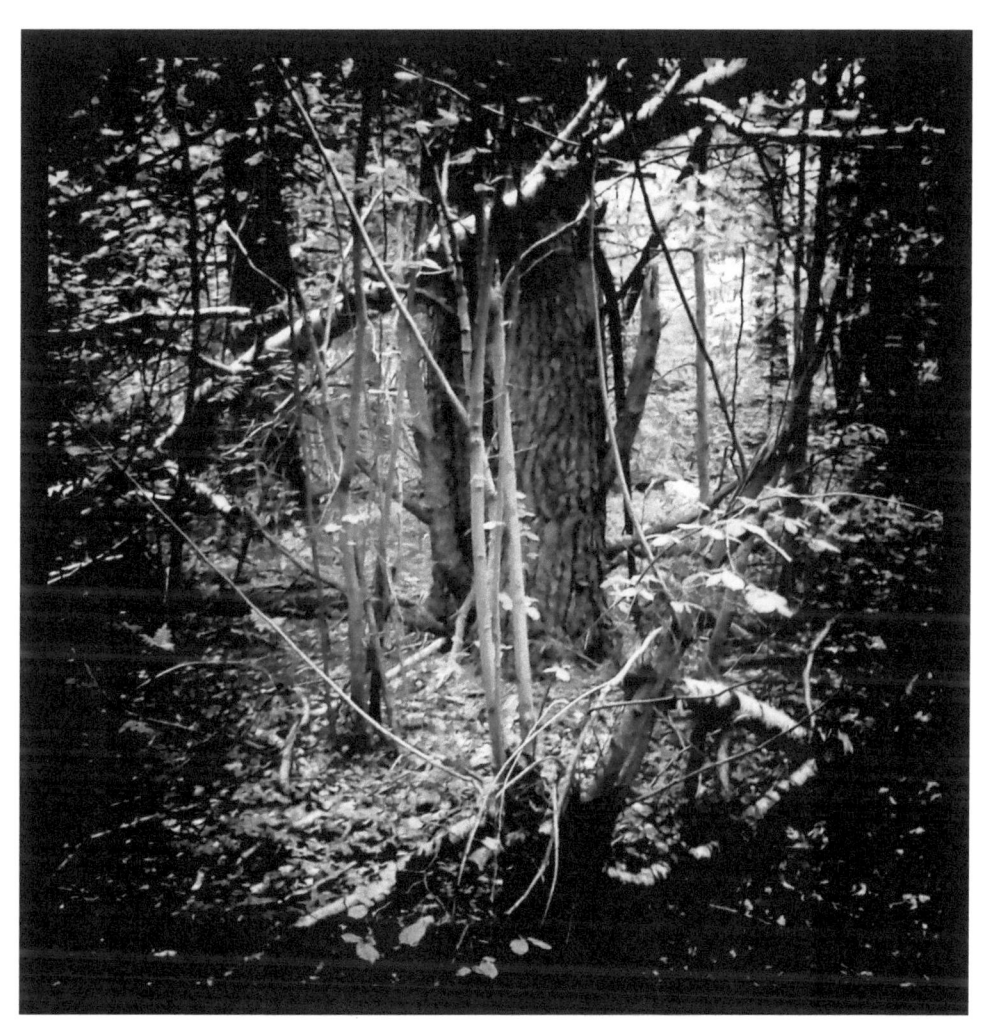

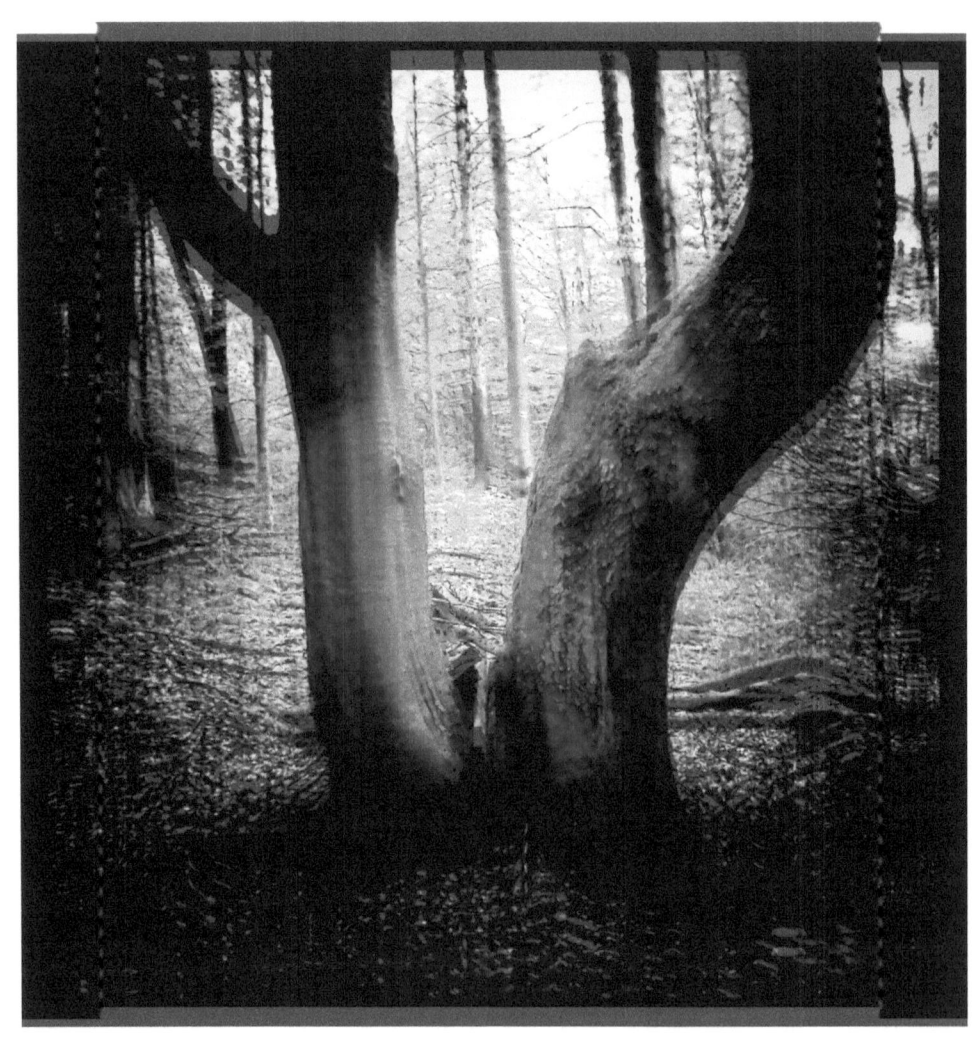

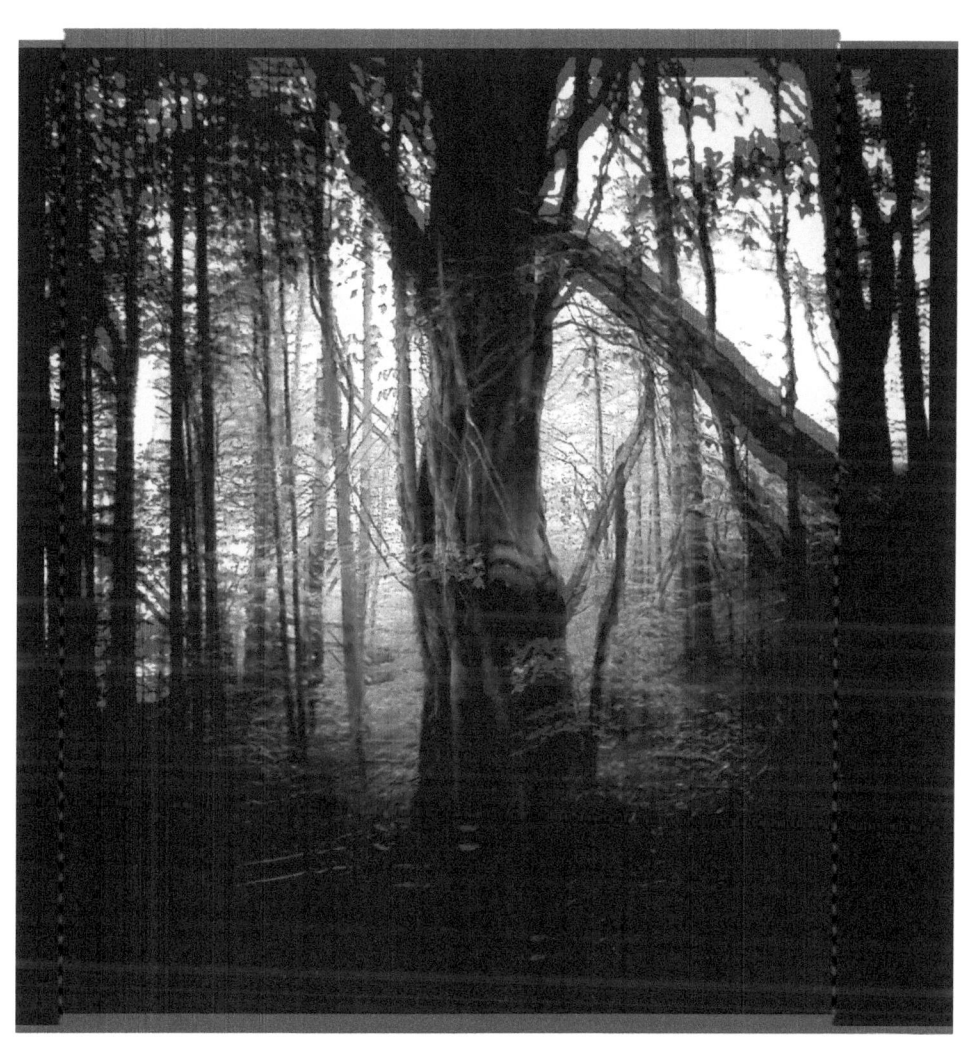

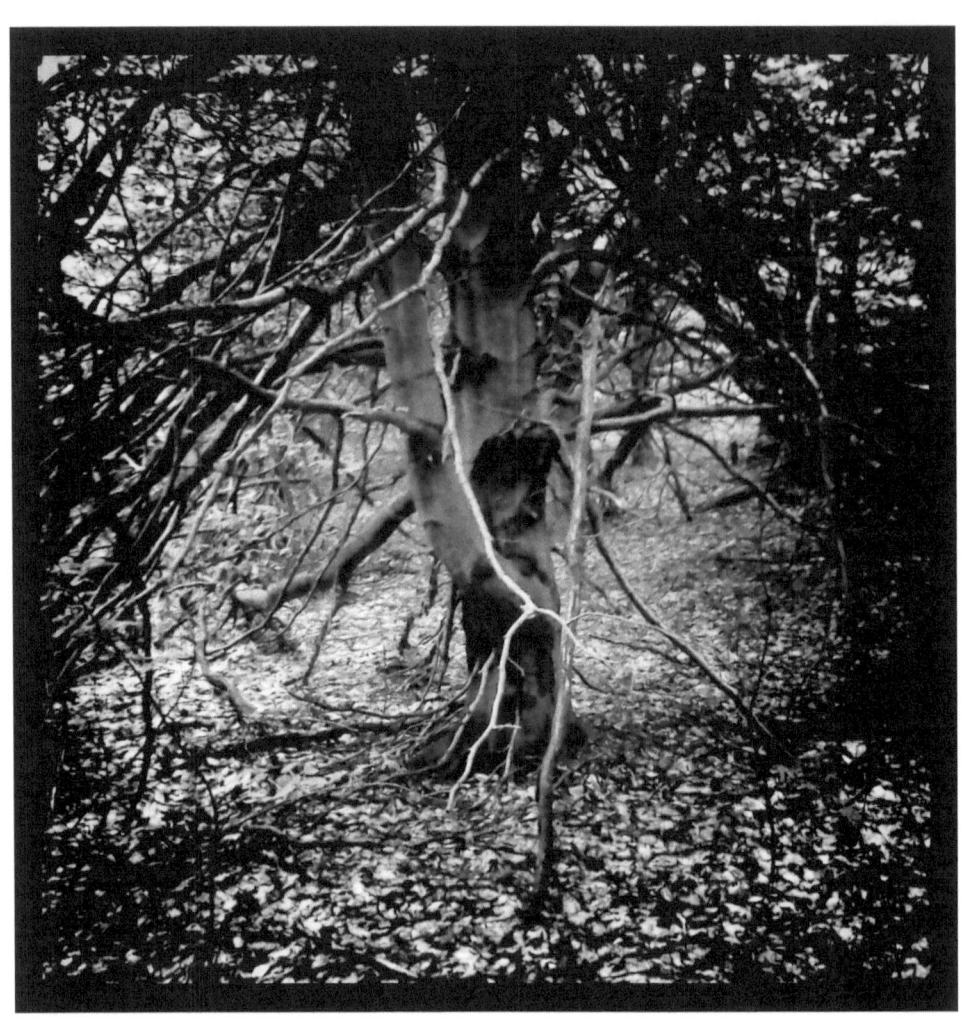

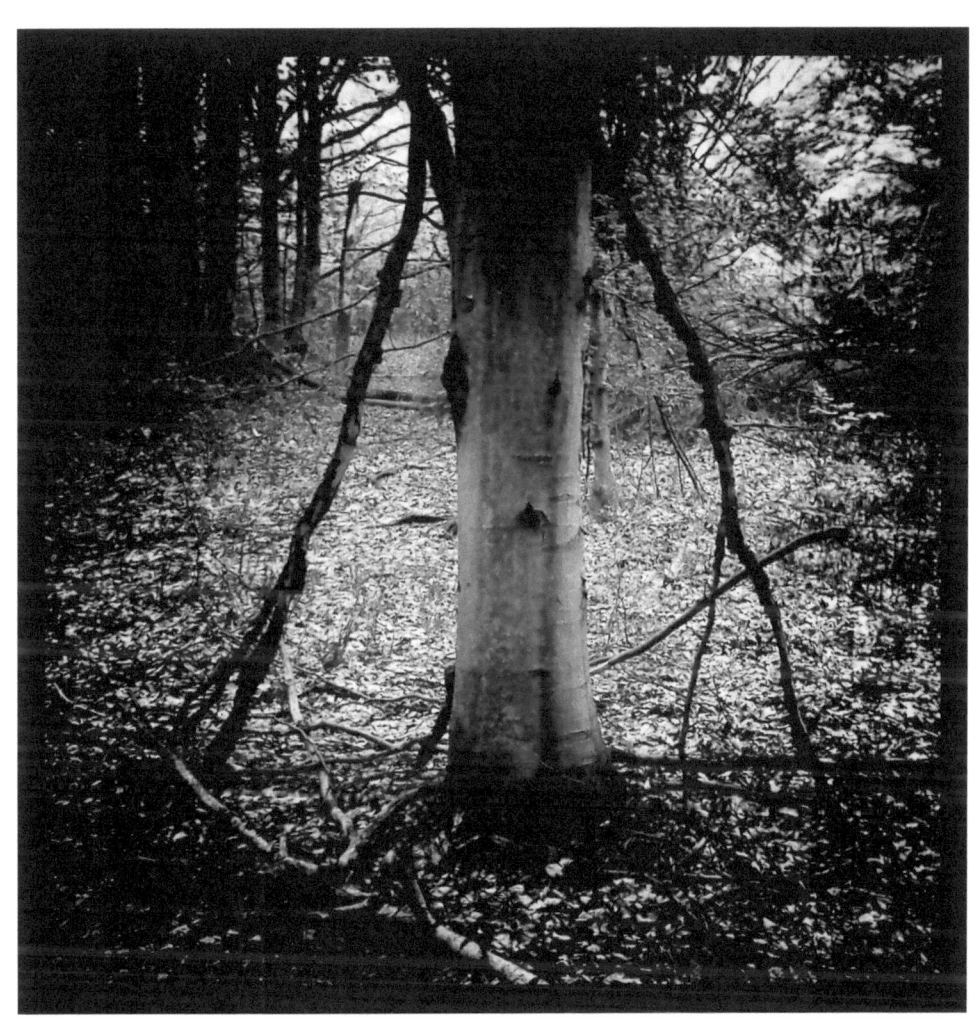

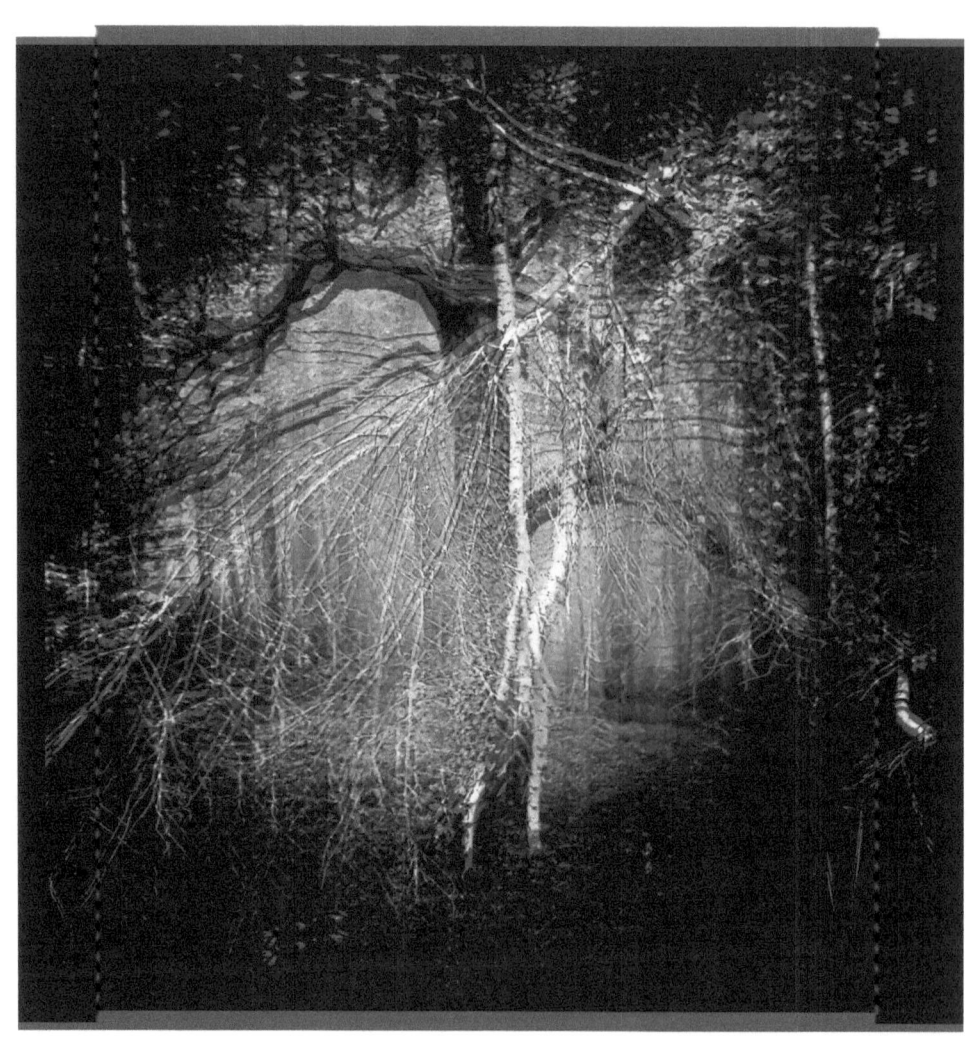

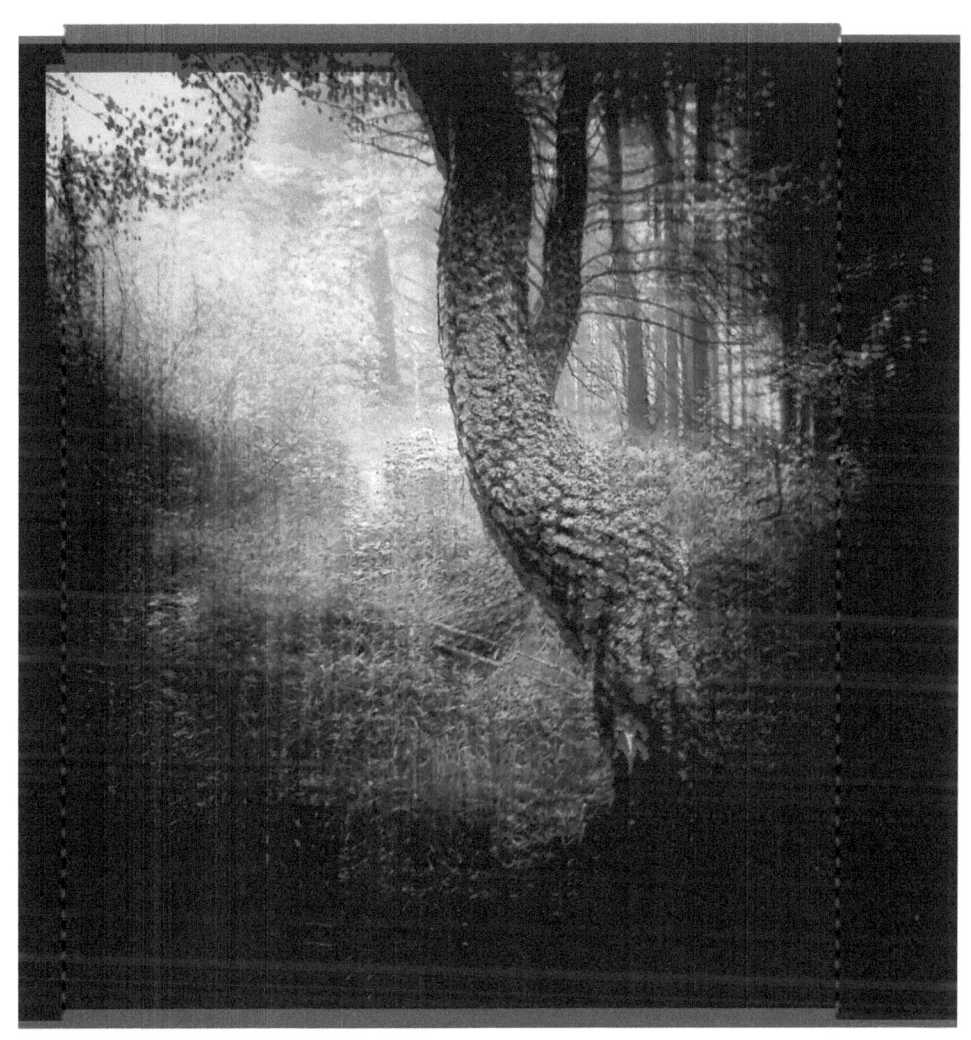

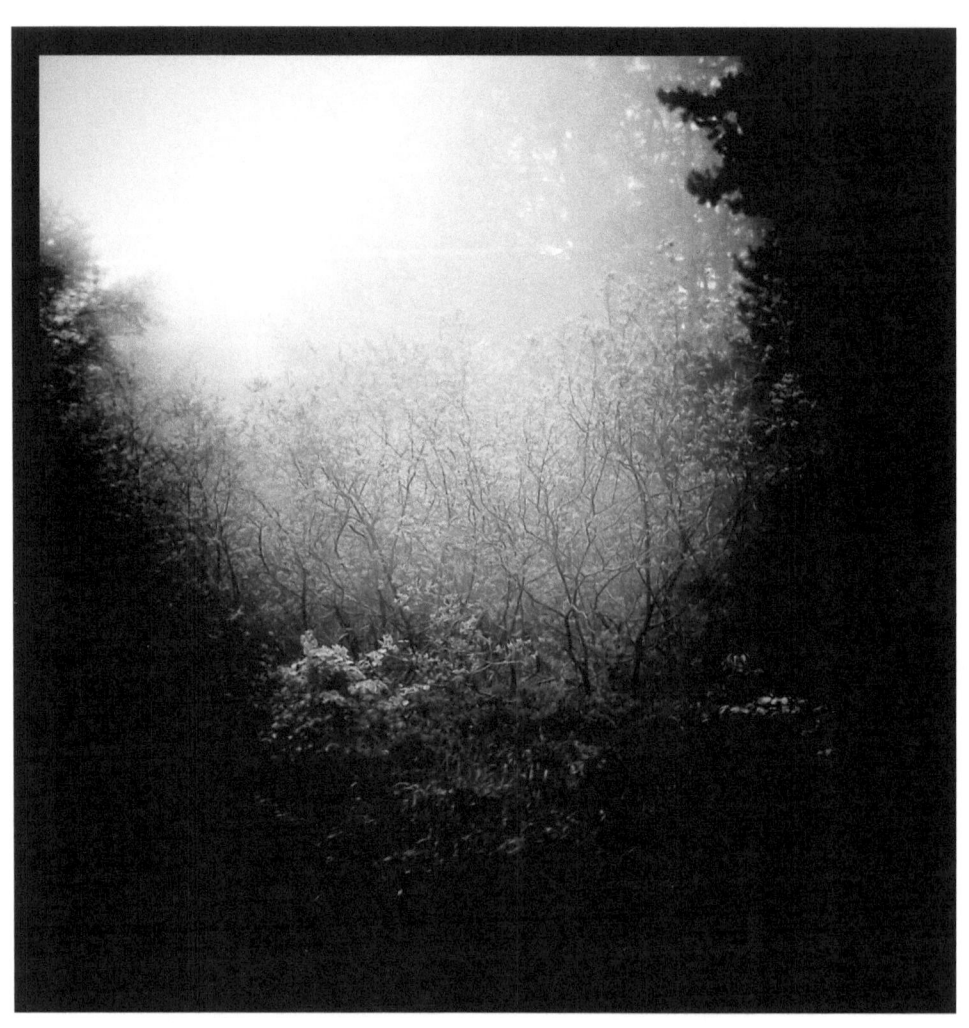

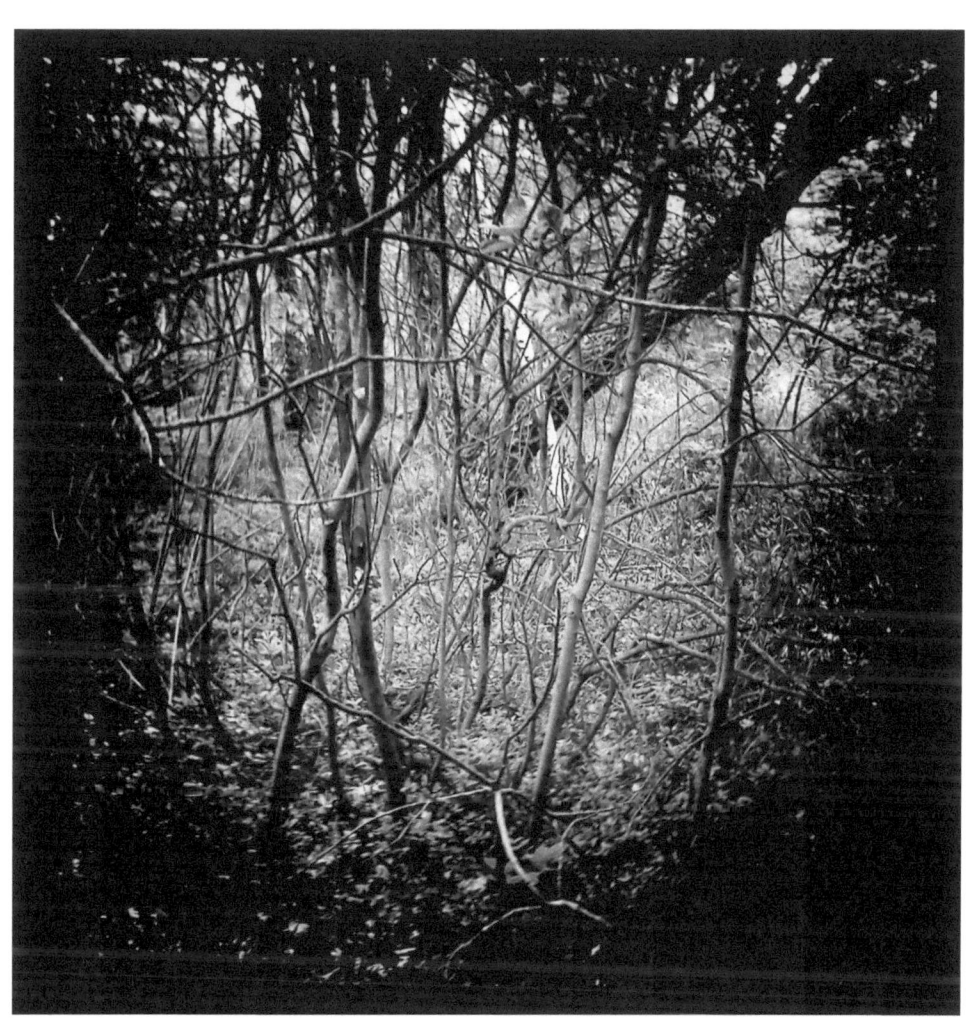

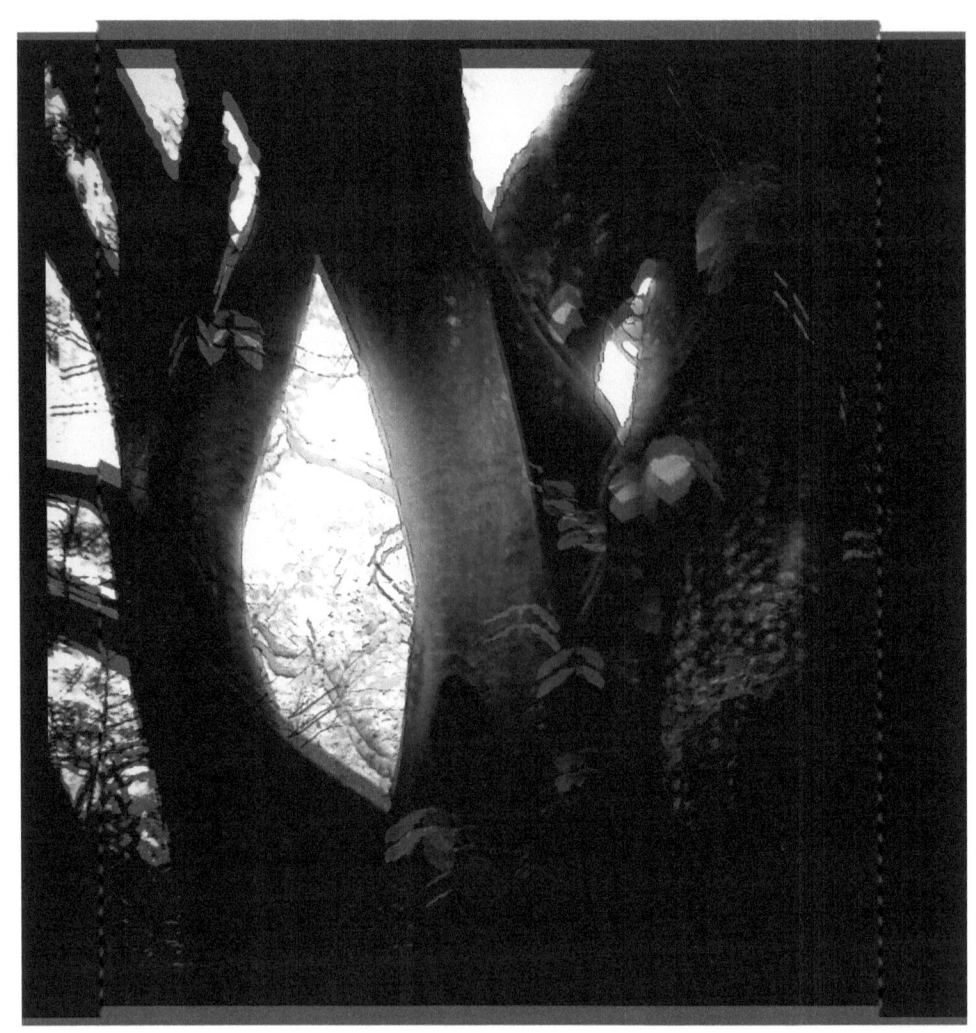

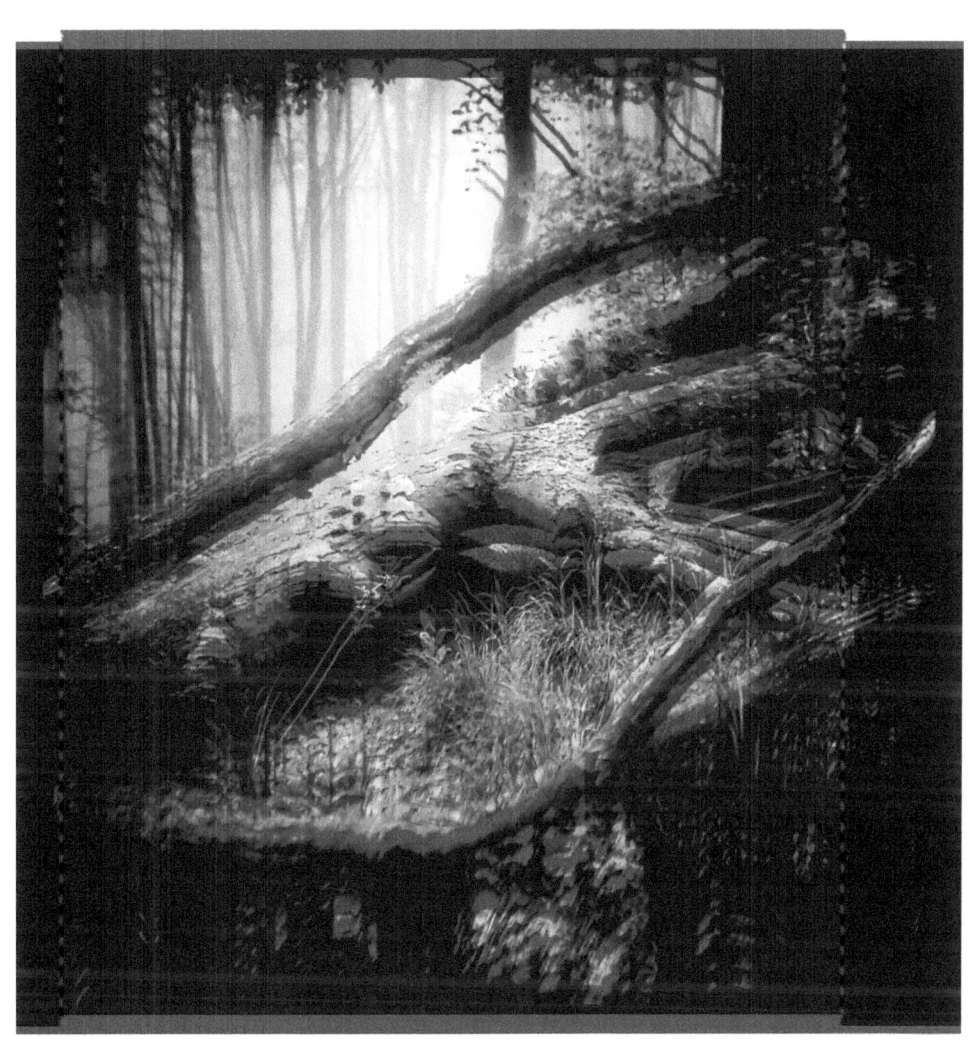

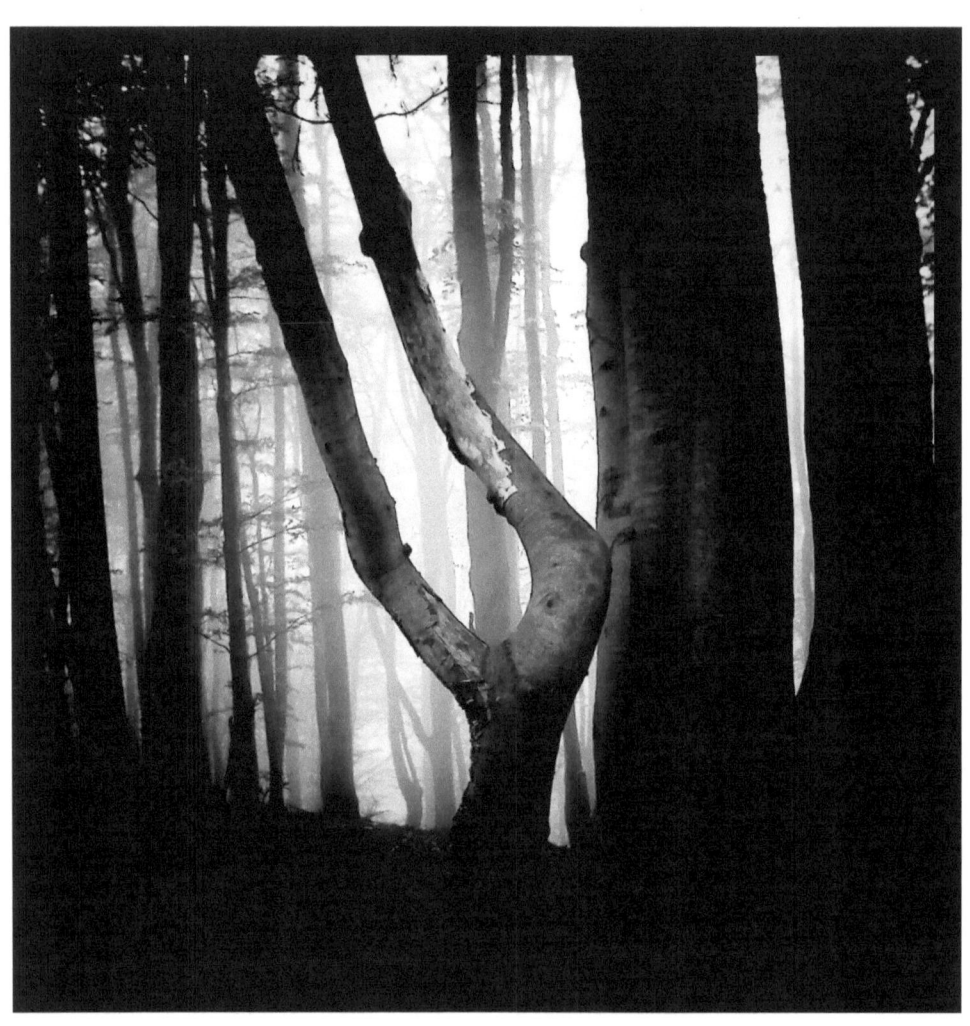

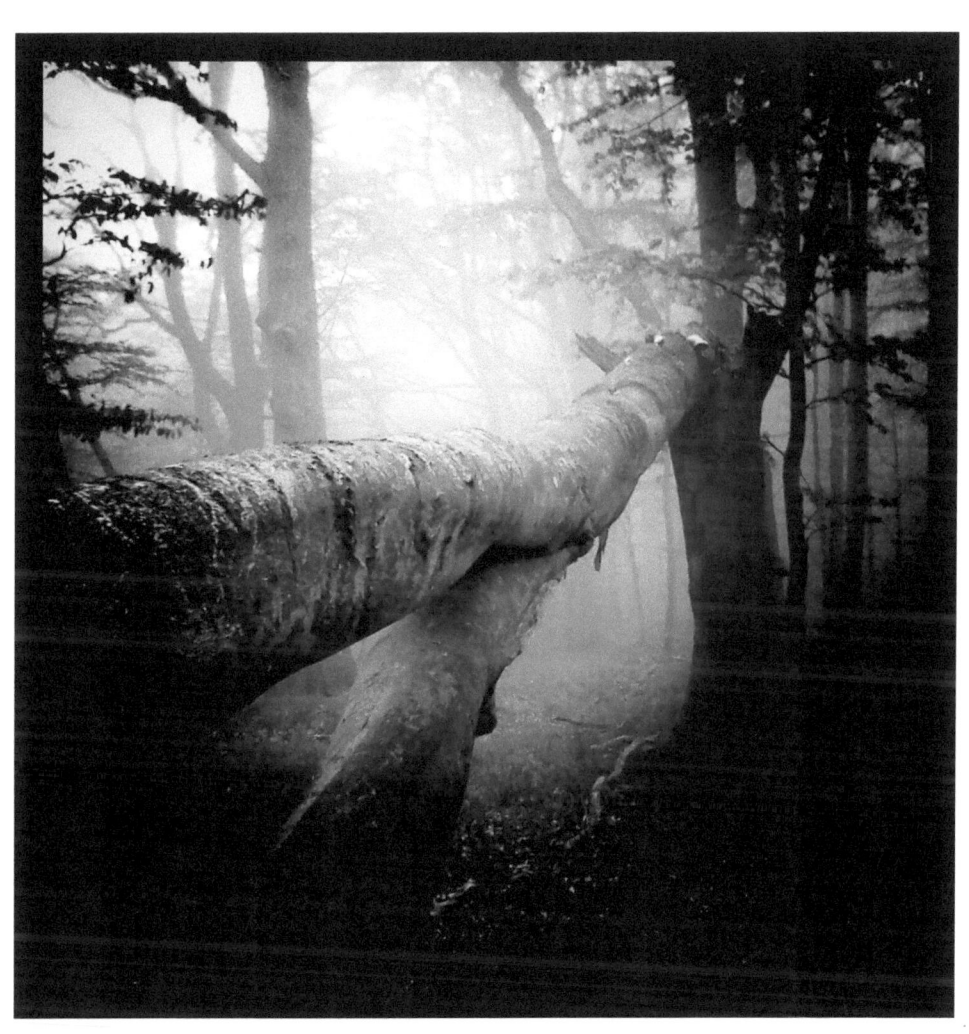

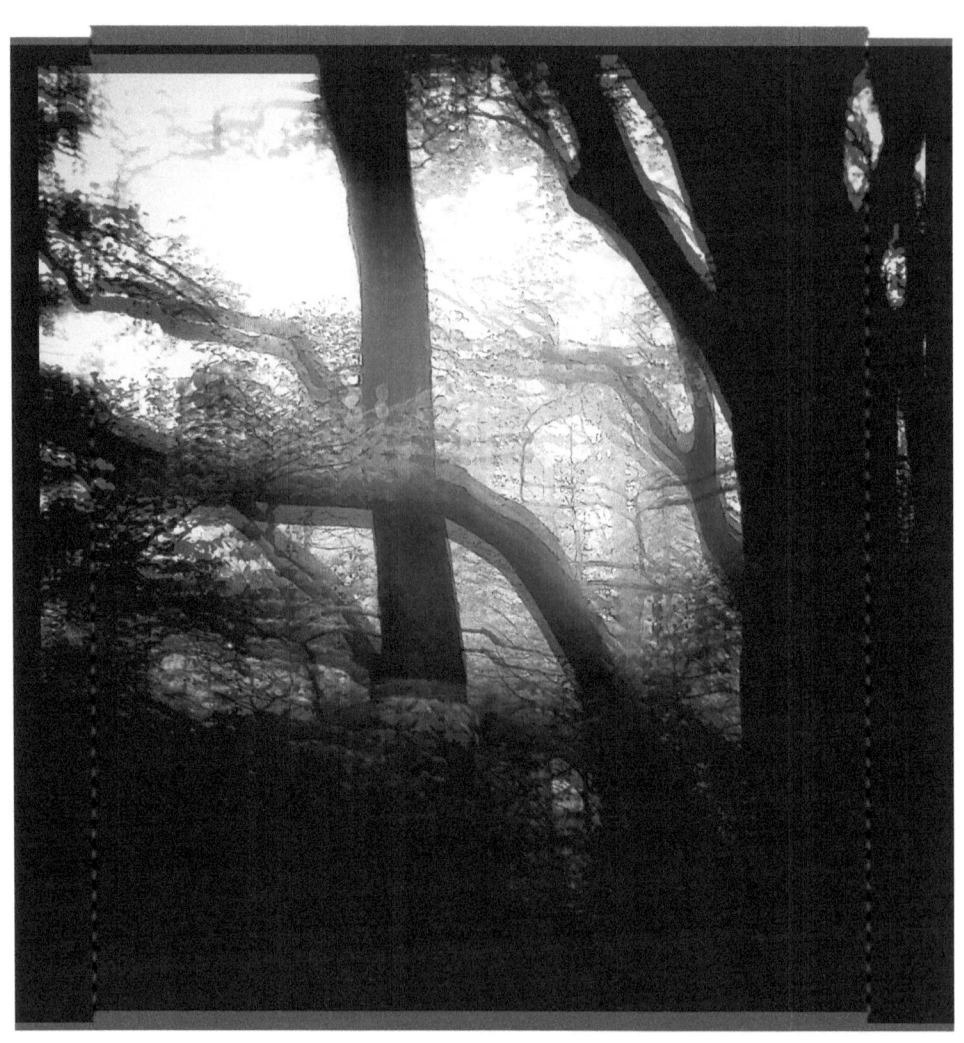

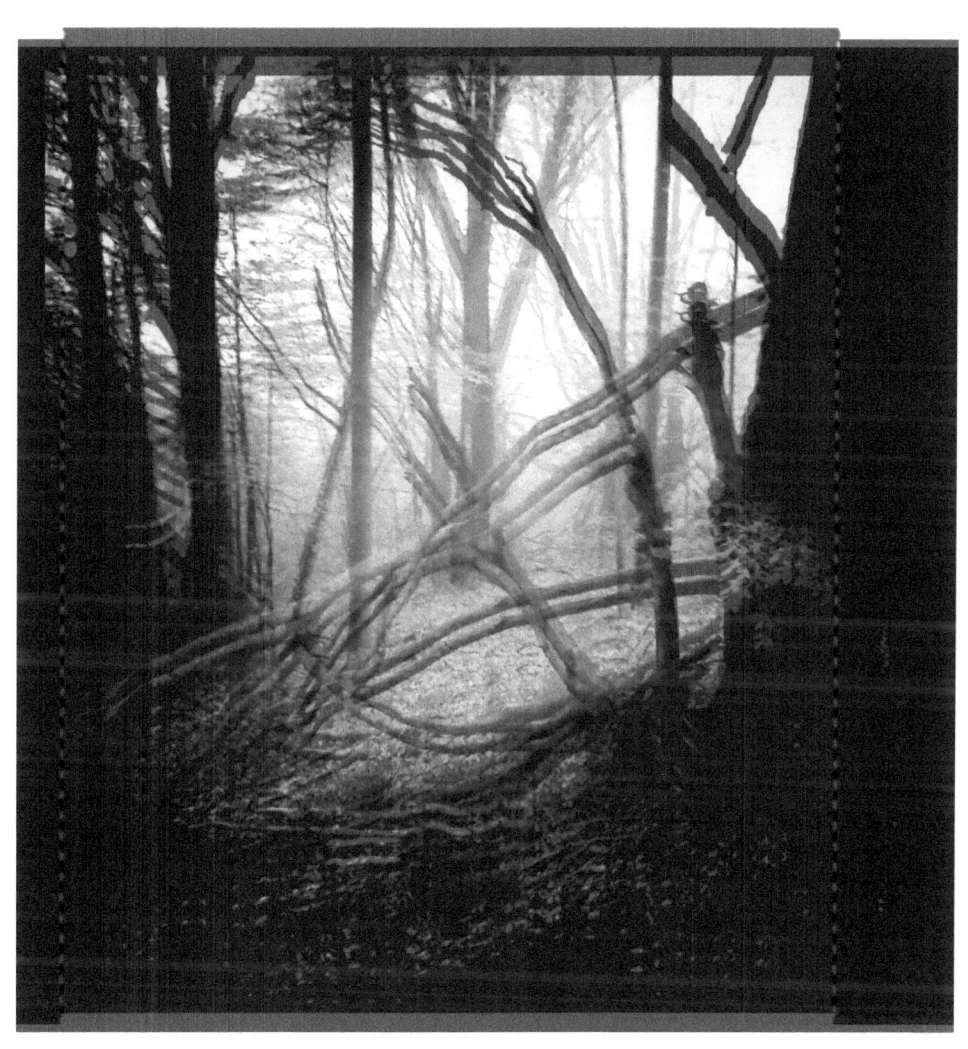

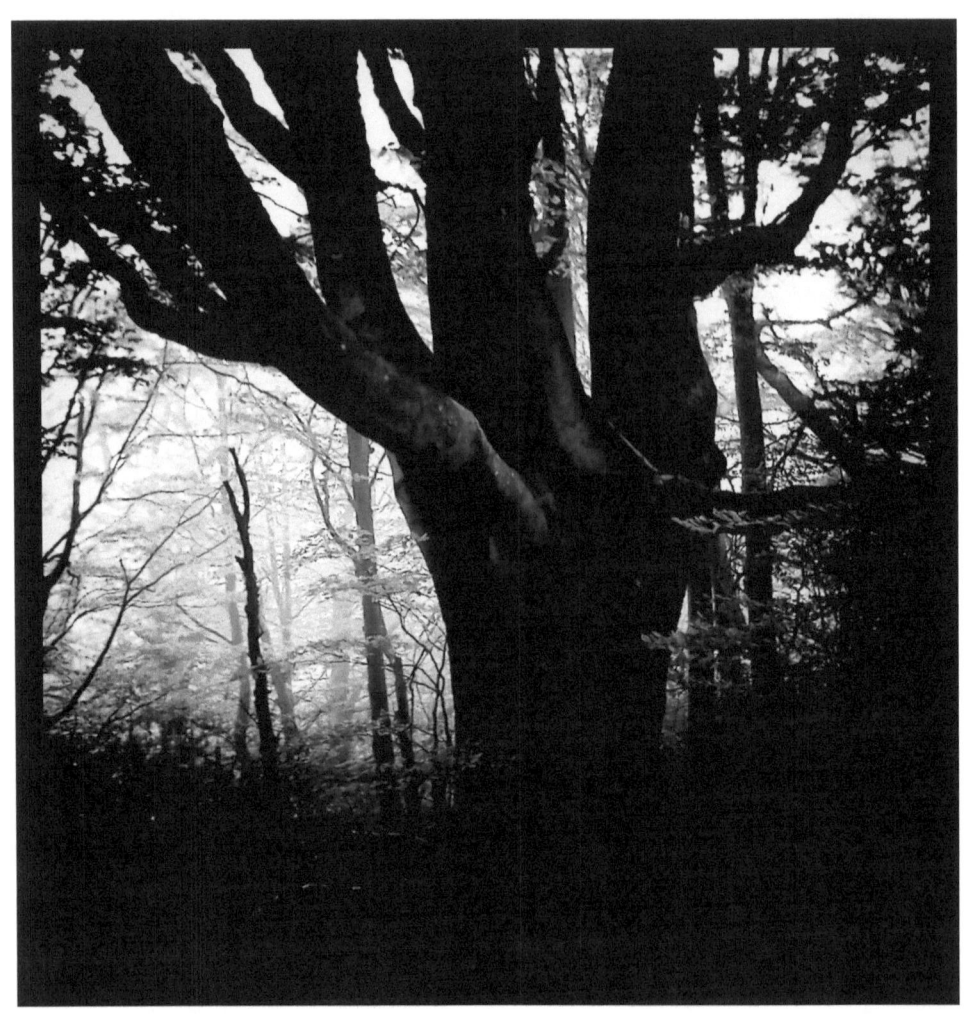

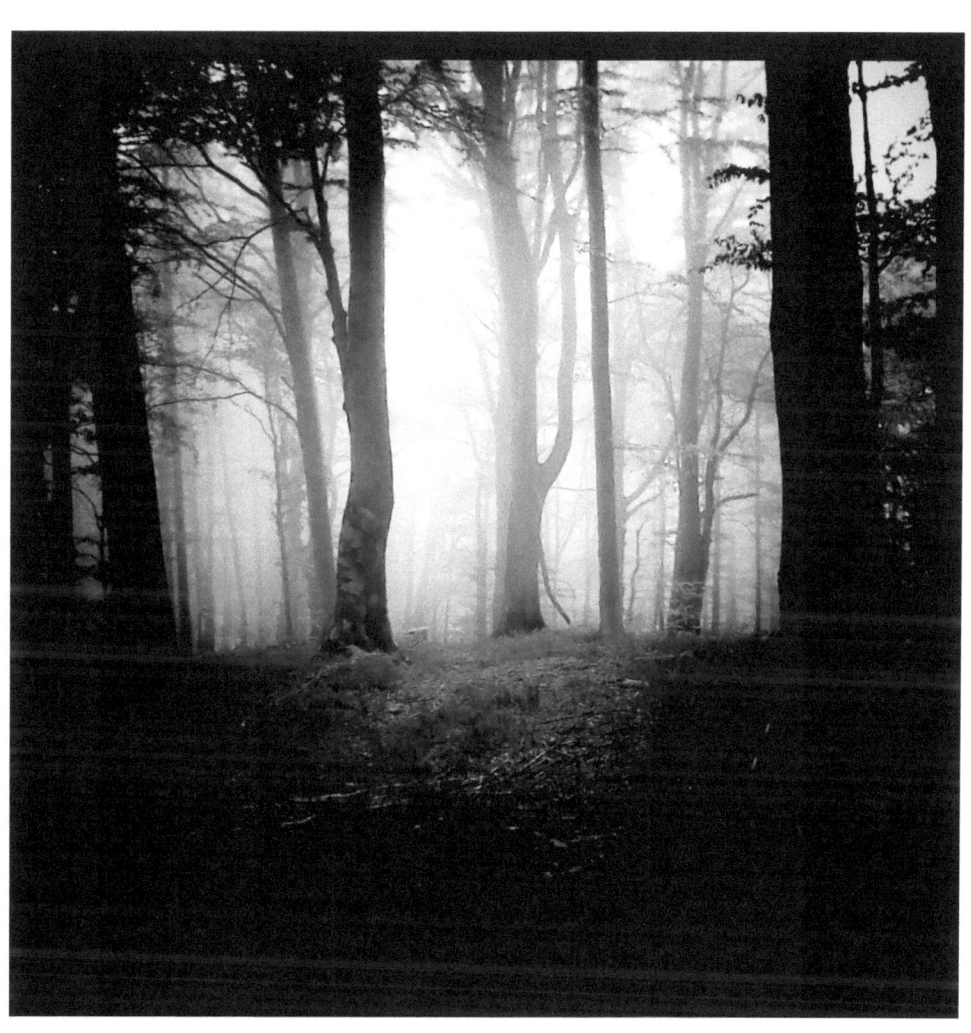

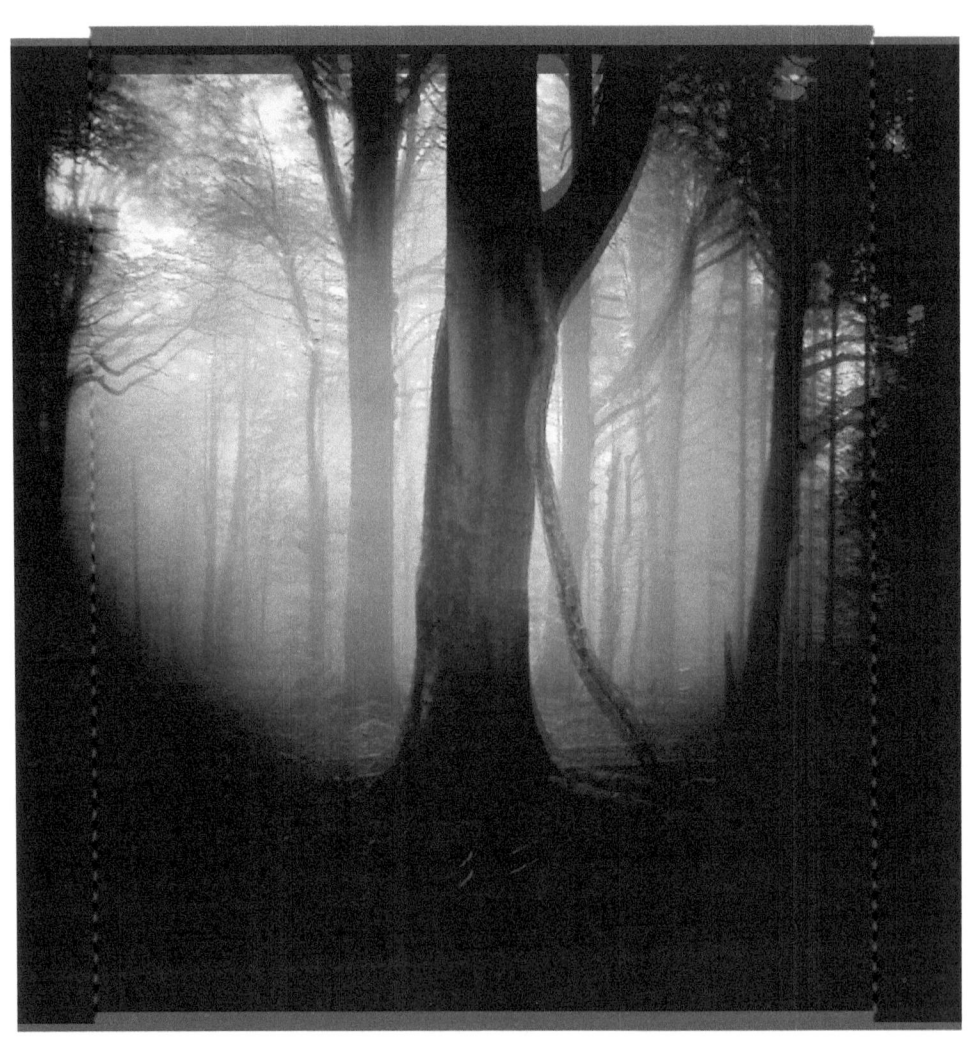

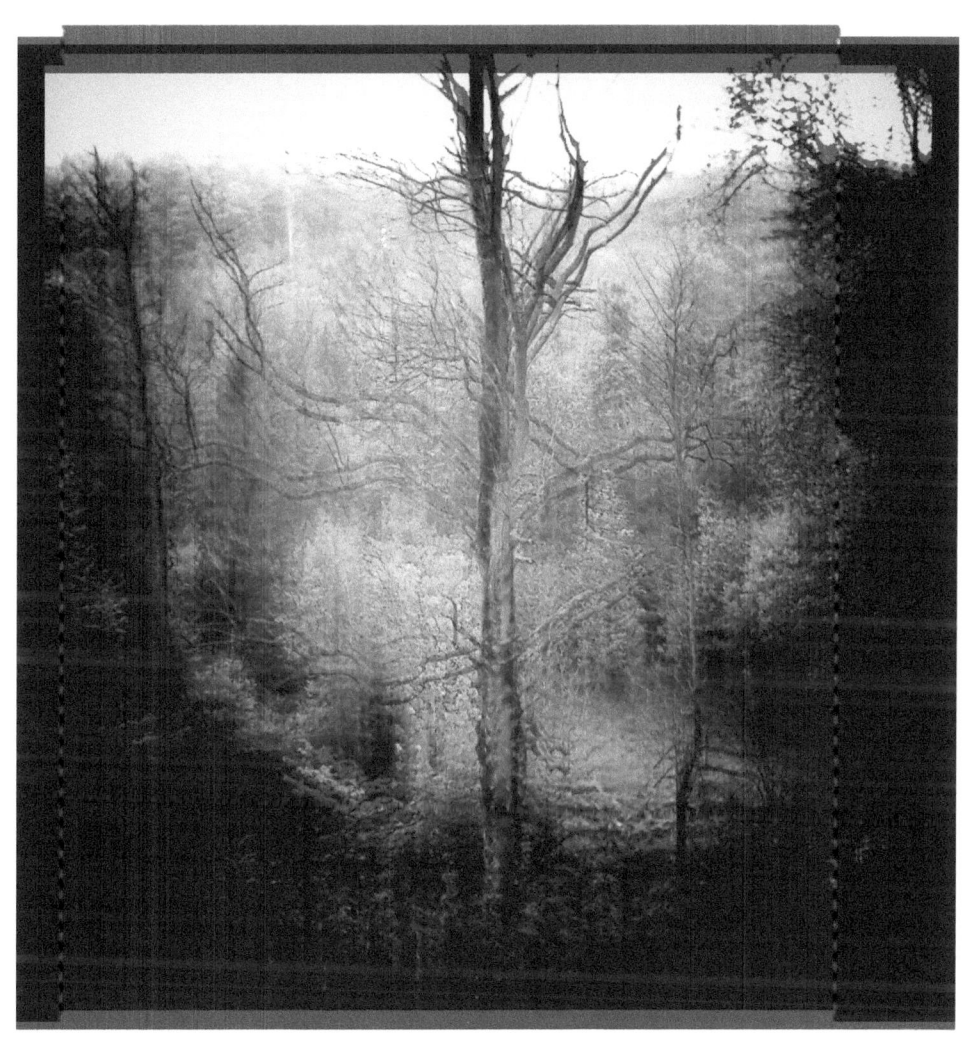

About author

I live in Poland. I photographed for many years and photography has been in the centre of my professional life since 2005. I am active at in many areas of photography: theater, fashion, street, document.
I realized several photo projects.
In 2012 and 2018 I was a stipendist of the minister of culture in Poland. My photos have featured in many publications and I have produced artwork and promotional images for artists, theatres and newspapers. I was exhibited in various exhibitions in Poland mostly in Katowice.

e-mail: jaceklidwin@wp.pl
phone: +48 663 184 900

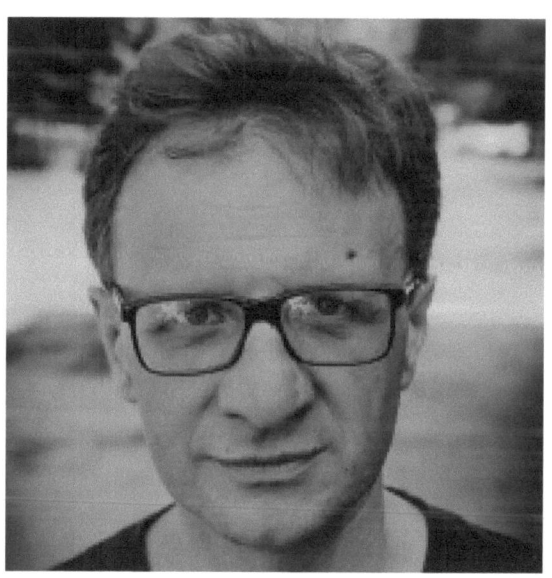

Stipends
Polish Ministry of Culture stipends:
2012 – Simply Stories – photographic project
2018 – Forgotten lives – photographic project
Marshal of The Silesian Voivodeship stipends in the field of culture:
2008 – Fragments of Ancient Names – Jewish cemeteries in Silesian Voivodeship – photographic project
2011 – A photo album about theater festivals A Part from 1998 to 2011
2014 – Ecce Homo – photographic project about homeless people
Individual exhibitions in Katowice in Poland
2003 – The Photographs That Were Taken in Szopienice – street photography
2008 – Unknown People – street photography
2009 – Human, space, light – theatrical photography at Roundabout Art Gallery
2009 – Unknown People – street photography
2010 – Packaging for the People – fashion photography
2011 – Fragments of Ancient Names – Jewish cemeteries in Silesian Voivodeship at The Archdiocesan Museum
2011/2012 – Presentation of the book about the festival A Part at Polish Radio Building

Book credits

Photos and texts: Jacek Lidwin

Cover and interior page layauts: Jacek Lidwin

Published by Jacek Lidwin

Copyright © 2020 by Jacek Lidwin

www.ingramcontent.com/pod-product-compliance
Lightning Source LLC
Chambersburg PA
CBHW051926210526
45473CB00006B/2144